Shadowbirds

Shadowbirds

A QUEST FOR RAILS

WILLIAM BURT

LYONS & BURFORD, PUBLISHERS

Design by Catherine Lau Hunt

Printed in the United States of America

10 9 8 7 6 5 4 3 2 1

Burt, William, 1948–
    Shadowbirds : a quest for rails / William Burt.
       p.   cm.
    Includes bibliographical references (and index.
    ISBN 1-55821-293-0
    1. Black rail—United States. 2. Yellow rail—United States. 3. Burt, William, 1948–   —Journeys—United States.   4. United States— Description and travel.   I. Title
QL696.G876B87   1994
598.3'1—dc20   94-1424
                                                                      CIP

CONTENTS

For my son Adam

Shadowbirds

ACKNOWLEDGMENTS

First of all, and most of all, it is S. Dillon Ripley whom I want to thank, for his keen encouragement of my photographic chases after those birds we both admire. It has been my privilege twice now to join him in producing articles on rails for *Smithsonian* magazine; and it was he who first suggested that I write a book about these curious marshland personalities. I'm not sure that the present volume is exactly what he had in mind, but I hope that he is pleased.

Roger Tory Peterson, too, has encouraged my photographic exploits, and has long provided inspirational example, as of course he has to many others.

Of those who took time to read the manuscript and comment I'm grateful first of all to David Burt, my uncle and my friend, who read it through at several stages of its being and urged me on. Shannon Davies, too, was most encouraging; she read through two drafts and offered helpful insights, especially with regard to biographical research on Reverend Peabody. Publisher Peter Burford has provided editorial care and wisdom, and at all times has been a pleasure to work with on this project. Others who read the work and commented were Dr. Bruce M. Beehler and Nancy Kerr Butler, and I thank them.

To Harold Shapiro I am ever thankful, for his expertise in the matter of photographic lighting. Without his help enabling the design of special equipment, my nocturnal pictures would be much poorer things, if they would be at all.

To Nathalie Paddon I'm thankful for her steadfast care in typing and retyping the manuscript, with that merciless eye of hers for spelling errors.

I'm grateful to all who helped in my search for clues to Reverend Peabody's life—particularly to Jean Bordner Braley of Shenandoah, Iowa, who actually knew Mr. Peabody and most generously gave over to me those of this books and letters in her possession. There is quite a little story to our connecting in this regard. Late one night she thought long about the minister from Kansas, recalled him vividly as she had not done in years, and then next day she chanced to see his name in the pages of a journal she seldom even opens: it was my little long-shot advertisement, placed in the hope of finding some soul somewhere who might remember him.

Ray Quigley of Hemet, California, gave freely of what material of Peabody's he had; and Marion Mengel at the University of Kansas Museum of Natural History kindly afforded access to those of his effects kept there, mostly photographs. Thanks also to the following, more or less chronologically, for providing other biographical bits and pieces: Helen Pearce of the Blue Rapids Public Library, Blue Rapids, Kansas; Warren Taylor, Special Collections Librarian, Topeka Public Library; Tamar Danufsky, at the Santa Barbara Museum of Natural History in California; Lloyd Kiff, Director, the Western Foundation of Vertebrate Zoology at Los Angeles; Ron Kaufman, of the Topeka Zoological Park; Frank Werner, of the Polk County Historical Society, Balsam Lake, Wisconsin; Stanley Peabody, of Amery, Wisconsin; Laurie Lewis, of the Shawnee County Probate Department, Topeka, Kansas; Pam Henson and Susan Glenn, of the Smithsonian Institution Archives, Washington, D.C.; Karen Stevens, at the Academy of Natural Sciences in Philadelphia; Mark Barrow, of the Department of the History of Science, Harvard University, and Robert Young of Harvard's Museum of Comparative Zoology Library; Eleanor McLean, at the Redpath Library, McGill University, Montreal; Dr. Tex Sordahl, at the Hoslett Museum of Natural History, Luther College, Decorah, Iowa; and Dr. Dean Amadon, of the American Museum of Natural History, New York City. And thanks to Al Mueller, Ornithology Librarian at the Peabody Museum of Natural History, Yale University, for facilitating my search through the periodical collections there.

Thanks to Dr. Sordahl, aforementioned, at Luther College, for use of the portrait of Reverend Peabody on page 131. And thanks to Allen Clark of Old Saybrook, Connecticut, for the photograph of his great grandfather, Judge John N. Clark, on page 26.

Lastly I want to thank my friends in North Dakota who

helped steer me toward Reverend Peabody's revered "Big Coulee": Del Hesse, Leon Arnold, Harold Alexander, and Edmond Gumeringer, all of Esmond and thereabouts—and Clarence Jensen, whom I was privileged to know just briefly, for he has since passed away; and Gary Huschle of the U.S. Fish and Wildlife Service at Devil's Lake. And thanks to Maureen Rodgers of the B. J. Hales Museum of Natural History at Brandon University, Brandon, Manitoba, for her enthusiastic help in acquainting me with that region.

INTRODUCTION

This book is about a quest for photographs of two birds, the black rail and the yellow rail: two shadowy little birds of the dark that live in marshes and are very, very hard to find—and harder still to photograph.

Rails are curious characters. Unbirdlike, they are fleet on foot and clumsy in the air; they keep to the thick of marshes, where they live their lives unseen. Chicken-like—"mudhens," or "marsh hens," they are called colloquially—they are awkward, undeveloped-looking creatures that nonetheless are the very wiliest of birds. Rails are prowlers in places of mud and shadow, slinkers in the reeds and grass, jittery nondescripts that shrink from view and slip silently away.

In North America there are six kinds of rails: the rich-brown king rail, of inland and brackish eastern marshes, and its paler, greyer salt marsh counterpart the clapper rail—these two are the largest of the group, nearly as big as chickens, and are now considered "forms" of a single species; the sora rail, of fresh marshes, most common in the northern prairie states and provinces, and the widespread Virginia rail, of marshes almost everywhere, both intermediate in size; and, lastly, those two miniature members of the family, no bigger than songbirds, in a class quite by themselves, the black and the yellow rails: they are rare, and exceedingly choosy about where they live.

Unlikely subjects of the camera, you might suppose, these unprepossessing skulkers of the marshes. Indeed, why trouble yourself? There are certainly more lyrical, more beautiful things to photograph, like curving mountain streams or wind-driven grass, or springboks springing; why not one of these? Or if the subject must be birds, then why not something bright, like warblers, or resplendent and exotic like toucans? Or imposing, like hawks and owls? Why spend years in splashy, floundering pursuit of two small, stubby, chicken-shaped birds of unremarkable color that live their skulking lives beneath a screen of grass?

For the difficulty, of course, and for the fascination of it, if you happen to be fascinated. Rails are potently fascinating if you let them be, and I, for one, have let them be for years, ever since I first found them lurking in the fastness of Connecticut River cattails, during teenage explorations. I found them seldom, and by accident—the usual means for finding rails—but I found them just often enough to pique my curiosity incurably. I began to search for them, and for their nests, and for the fun

King Rail. Old Lyme, CT., June 1975

of it I tried to photograph them, with a 200 mm semi-telephoto lens of a brand I have never heard of since. I did get photographs of the common kinds of rails, mostly soras and Virginias, and my efforts were technically commendable sometimes, considering the nature of the birds; never, however, were they eloquent.

Then one day by accident I found a king rail's nest. Right at my feet a big brown bird jumped off its basketful of eggs and stood still, staring, engaging me like a warrior with feathers all puffed out and bristling, growling its animosity. Pictorially, the moment was a magic one. Under a leaden sky in soft, saturating light this bird stood fixed and menacing and regal. Racing past beyond him was the slanting dark green torrent of the grass, and clinging in the green were silvery, saw-toothed leaves of silverweed, bright and steadfast in the flow like riffles in a stream. He stood still and fierce, wings out; it was a gift, an accident, an opportunity to pluck . . . and I took it.

By this time I had photographed all the North American rails except for two, the black rail and the yellow. Could they, too, be found and photographed? It was an irresistible idea, and following this king rail gift I felt I might find luck enough to do so. Off I went, then, to Maryland and then to Minnesota, North Dakota, and Manitoba; this book is about what happened there. It is about two birds, and this photographer's single-minded search for them, and for their nests; and it is about the places, too, and sometimes people, and adventures and misadventures along the way. And, increasingly, it is about a presence of the past, a turn-of-the-century naturalist whose footsteps I found myself retracing.

Two secret birds of far nocturnal meadows: what

dreamy things to quest for. Of all the many birds there are to photograph, no others are so mysterious, so magical—or so superbly difficult to find. There are no substitutes; no other, lesser birds will do.

I

Red Eyes Blazing

~ 1 ~

DORCHESTER COUNTY, MARYLAND
June, 1984

Late on a June night, the road from Vienna to Elliott Island is untraveled. In the headlights deer eyes glow, and a moth-chasing whip-poor-will streaks past. The air is heavy, sweet with honeysuckle: rounded tops of loblolly pine stand dark against a moon-bright sky. Passing, slowly, the ruins of a tumbledown farm building, I hear out the car window a quick spitted little song—a Henslow's sparrow? I stop. Henslow's it is: two of them, in a moonlit pasture, singing spiritedly but invisibly, indiscernible among the small, dark, billion heads of weeds. In the distance, strange southern frogs are jungle-honking.

I follow a narrowing road, a long, dark avenue through

Evening, along the Elliott Island road.

pinewoods that are forbiddingly still. A big owl coasts over the car. Along the road to either side are ditches full of dark water and cattail blades blue-green in the headlights. A raccoon, caught wading, looks up and turns away. The pines are towering, then gone—suddenly the world is bright and open; moonlight jiggles on the water, and dark grass extends forever.

I stop, turn off the car, and step out. I listen a little reluctantly, this first time, as if I don't really want to hear it. Not right away.

On ahead, again, I stop to listen. This time I'm trying—I'm straining—to hear the call, however faint. But there is none to hear. Not yet.

I'm listening for a bird I'll learn little about tonight, even should I find one—a bird much easier to hear than see. I'm listening for a bird no bigger than a sparrow, slate-black and speckled on the back with white. A dark little bird: dark and unobtrusive, except for its igneous red eyes; a bird of rarity, and microscopic beauty; the black rail.

It is a canny, quick-footed little bird—a "feathered mouse," in the words of ornithologist Alexander Sprunt, Jr., that spends its life in the fine grass of salt meadows. Its stealth is legendary, and it should be: the black rail is so secretive, so deftly elusive in its vast, green, filamentous world that a person can spend hours in a salt marsh every day, walking among these birds, and never catch sight of one. When approached it does not fly, like any usual bird; it slips away beneath the grass on foot—easily, imperceptibly, like a mouse.

Judge John N. Clark

Photograph courtesy of Allen Clark.

One man knew all about the mousiness of this creature, and he knew it long ago. He was Judge John N. Clark, and at Old Lyme, Connecticut, in 1884 he found the nest of a black rail by accident. He tried to match wits with the bird:

> *I . . . visited the nest about every half hour through the day, approaching it with every possible caution, and having a little tuft of cotton directly over the nest to indicate the exact spot: but although I tried from every quarter with the utmost diligence and watchfulness, I was never able to obtain the slightest glimpse of the bird—never perceived the slightest quiver of the surrounding grass to mark her movements as she glided away, and yet I found the eggs warm every time, indicating that she had but just left them.*

He never did see the parent bird.

What else should you know about this magician, this wizard of a bird? You should know about its calls. Were it not for its calls, it would be almost impossible to find.

The "song" of the male is a froggy, perfunctory *de-de-drr* repeated mechanically, with metronomic regularity, often for hours at a time and from a single spot. You hear it late at night, in spring and early summer. It has been found by enterprising birding fellows that a tape recording of this song, played back to a calling rail, will sometimes attract the bird. The tape is perceived to be an interloping male, and response can be strong; there are stories of defiant birds growling at their battery-powered adversaries, charging at them, even climbing on them and jabbing them with their beaks. So incensed was one bird by the machine, the story goes, that he excreted on it.

The call of the female is a dove-like cooing, and is very rarely heard. Other calls, rarer still, such as barks and clucks and weak windy whistles have been imputed to black rails; but their significance is quite unknown.

Masterful as they are at keeping out of sight, black rails are shrewder still, supremely so, when it comes to hiding their nests and eggs. On the east coast not a single nest has been found since 1953, when one was found by accident in Maryland. Not that there has been any lack of diligent and dedicated search. In 1967, during a study of salt-marsh sparrows on Long Island, two men named Post and Enders trapped and banded black rails in a marsh where calls were regularly heard at night. They searched thoroughly for nests of all bird species, but found none of this one.

More recently another man, John Weske, made black rails the subject of a Master's thesis, and he spent an entire summer studying them in the marshes at Elliott Island, Maryland, quite literally living among his subjects on the marsh, in a hunter's lodge from which he could hear them calling at night through each and every window. Meticulous searches were made for nests, especially where males were heard at night; four men spent two days assisting Weske in his search, and so did a Labrador retriever "with proven ability in finding duck nests." But not a nest was found. Says Weske:

> The link between the territorial singing male and the nest is perhaps the greatest mystery surrounding the black rail. No young were found, nor even an indication of a female bird being present on the marsh.

Black rails used to nest where I live, in Connecticut. I've always hoped to find them there. They are southern birds, favoring certain marshes on the eastern seaboard from New Jersey southward, and the farthest north they now occur is southeastern Long Island, at Oak Beach, where one or two are heard most years. But they did nest in Connecticut a century ago. At the mouth of the Connecticut River Judge Clark found and collected two nests, one at Old Lyme and another across the River at Saybrook, and he knew of three other nests collected thereabouts. For any species of rail, in an area as circumscribed as the Connecticut River estuary, five is a respectable number of nests to account for in a two-decade span; but five nests of the black rail is a sum that flabbergasts. How common they must have been.

On a calm spring night, from Smith's Neck Landing at Old Lyme you can listen across the channel to Great Island, exactly the salt meadow in which Judge Clark stooped to discover the nest of 1884. You can hear the ticking of clapper rails, the bubble and chatter of marsh wrens, and now and then the sneeze of a seaside sparrow. On such nights one hundred years ago the frog-like notes of yet another bird must commonly have sounded. . . . Judge Clark would have heard them, had he sat here late at night; but they sound no longer.

Three hundred miles south of Old Lyme, on the eastern shore of Chesapeake Bay, jutting between Fishing Bay and the Nanticoke River estuary, is a formidable tract of marsh, thirty square miles of needlerush and *Spartina*. Elliott Island, it is called; and here there still are such things as black rails. Here they can still be heard on June nights, and even seen sometimes, purportedly, when lured to a tape recording. Maybe they can be photographed, too. And maybe there are nests to find: dogged search might turn one up, it seems to me. It's not unthinkable; they do build such things.

~ 2 ~

Still no calls, no black rails; only marsh wrens, and frogs, and a single sora rail. A barn owl hisses in the distant dark. Of course it should not be immediate, or easy; and it is not.

Eight years ago I made a try for Maryland black rails. It was a halfhearted try, admittedly, for I brought company along, a wife and a sister-in-law; and you don't do that if you want to find black rails. I have this memory of standing and listening beside the road while the girls sat grimly in the car, with windows cranked up tight, mosquitoes pattering against the glass. They thought it a dreadful sound, almost as dreadful as the whine of those at large inside the car. The motel that night was awful, too; the trip was a fiasco, and a short one.

More stops to listen . . . again, again, dutifully every half mile. The strange southern frogs: they are green tree frogs—"cow bell" tree frogs, colloquially. At a distance, indeed, they sound like clanking cowbells, but closer they *honk:* a little like geese, and a little like something in the jungle. Far out here on the marsh they are becoming fewer, but honking little colonies do persist and when you are near one you hear nothing else. So you move on, if you're listening for rails.

Marsh wrens, on the other hand, are everywhere. I hear the hard, sharp notes of a sedge wren: good thing to hear. Uncommon. But why are there no black rails? I'm ready now. For two hours now my patience has been saintly . . . but it is dissolving fast. How will I ever *see* the bird, let alone photograph it, and photograph it well, if I can't even hear it? The whole idea is losing spirit. The reedy cheer of wrens seems ordinary now, even irritating. Conspiratorial, that's what it is; they conspire to exclude the rarer, less assertive voice. They are jeering, cachinnating hecklers. It's their fault.

Surprise: a car. Parked beside the road is a finned old Plymouth and beyond it, in the marsh, are two young figures holding flashlights.

The urge is to intrude. I park ahead, grab my light, and walk back along the road. Holding the flashlights are two boys, and near them *de-de-drrs* are plain to hear. "Is that a rail you have, or a tape?"

"It's a tape, but there's a rail out here. Come on out, if you want."

On the marsh between them their tape is playing. And beyond, not far, from deep in the grass comes a series of protracted whines, like those of a perturbed vireo; they accelerate and run together in a wren-like chatter. The boys say that the rail has been calling for an hour in this way, but has refused to show. Occasionally a muffled *de-de-drr* is given, almost at the feet of one of us, but the source cannot be seen.

Forty minutes pass. "I see him," gasps one of the boys as his light moves slowly in the direction of my feet. Then I catch sight of the dark, slender form as it threads its way through the lower grasses; seconds later I lose him. Next comes an exclamation from the other boy, who has not yet had a look—he now has a light on him. We converge, and as we all watch the shadowy skulker climbs upward and emerges, transfigured, upon the surface of the grass; he stands immobile for the moment, elegant, sparrow-tiny and proud, magnificent with neck outstretched and red eyes blazing in our lights. Suddenly then, with a burst of wings he jumps up and flies fumblingly away. There is handshaking and jubilation as we make our way back to the road.

Departing, the boys are giddy with success, still reeling; needing to thank somebody they thank me, as if my presence had been something crucial. They are headed back to Pennsylvania, whence they came. Alone, I continue the dark drive across the marsh, thankful for my headlight beams; mists hang over the road in sheets that part submissively, eerily as I drive right through. The road runs straight as a light beam for a mile or two, then winds around through thickety copses, in one of which a yellow-breasted chat sings antically right by my window as I pass him by; then it breaks out into open marsh again. Here in this one rich plat of marsh several rails are calling. And one of them is provocatively close to the road, in a bristly band of cordgrass: a good prospect for photography. I assemble the apparatus and make a delicate approach, then set the tape player down, gently, and start it up. Here we go. He speeds up his call excitedly, then stops altogether, growls, and resumes calling at a relaxed and automated rate. For one full hour I stand in place with flash units charged, green-blinking, ready to fire, but it will not happen. He will not be seduced away from cover.

Drugged with weariness and exhilaration, both, I drive away at four AM, stopping once again at the abandoned farm, now dark and silent and asleep, no longer moon-inspired; no tree frogs nor Henslow's sparrows call. Far off is the rollicking song of a chuck-will's-widow.

What a bird, what eyes. It is the eyes that haunt you; those blazing eyes.

What is it about rails? They would seem deliberately designed to be displeasing, these dull-colored, songless birds that live in inconvenient places.

You don't find them printed on postage stamps or postcards or place mats or on the pages of calendars, in company with cardinals and egrets and owls. Most people have never even heard of rails (of feathered ones, at least). Nonetheless, to those who know them they are items of irresistible appeal.

It is the elusiveness, the inaccessibility, that fascinates. Rails are masters of their unsolid haunts, haunts in which one's human body is outsize and overweight and in the way. We wander into marshes to become helpless and unable, to flounder and splash and stick and stall and curse and drag ourselves about while blithely around us, unseen, like live shadows the rails skip weightlessly away over water and mud and slick floating green plants, hooking with long curved toes the grass and streaking through their jungle world with frictionless and unimpeded speed, playfully, free and fluent in their element as eels among kelps, as swallows and falcons that swim the air.

Rails outstep us, and outwit us easily, naturally, without the need to try. In rails we "witness our limits transgressed," as Thoreau said, writing of wild things.

Elliott Island marshes are primitive and wild. They are undefaced by the neat parallel surgery of ditching that has been inflicted upon more accessible, more easily emasculated wetlands; and they are unsullied by the usual weekend litter, or creeping landfill heaps, or spilling-over industry. They are intact and uninsulted, as marshes ought to be. And they are vast: they seem virtually unbounded, when you are in their midst, yielding only to fuzzy, faraway treelines in the north and east, and yielding elsewhere only to the sky. Miles apart are bold, lone stands of club-topped pines, hazy and distorted in the summer vapors. It might be Africa—these might be acacias on the hot dry plain; there might be giraffes. . . .

Where under the sun do you begin to look for the nest of a black rail? In the first place, I need to decide upon a specific type of marsh: there are several here at Elliott Island, and there are whole square miles of each. Most prevalent are two: the *Spartina alterniflora* marshes, wet, muddy, and loosely populated with tall, coarse blades, relatively unconcealing acres; and the dense *Spartina patens* marshes, airy, aromatic meadows of soft, fine grasses matted and knotted by the wind, sometimes pure and yellow-green and sometimes mixed with bluish "spikegrass" *(Distichlis),* where a little wet, or with *alterniflora,* where wetter still. Less extensive, but characteristic nonetheless, are two others: the "three-square" bulrush marshes, waist-high stands of stiff triangular stalks treed at the ends with blades that droop; and the forbidding needle-rush marshes, most dread of all, bleak, sere-looking acres that you crash your way across with injury, chastized constantly by steely speartips that pierce your pants and flesh. Needlerush is not where you look for nests, I'm sure of that.

Where *do* you look, Judge Clark?

> *This nest was situated about forty rods back from the shore of the river, on the moist meadow, often overflowed by the spring tides. The particular spot had not been mowed for several years, and the new grass, springing up through the old, dry, accumulated growths of previous years, was thick, short, and not over eight or ten inches in height, a fine place for Rails to glide unseen among its intricacies.*

In mixed grasses old and new, then, the judge would have me look. But there were others who found black rail nests: Turner McMullen, most notably, who found them in southern New Jersey sixty years ago in *Spartina patens* meadows, by flipping up the old matted-down grass with a stick. "Show me a salt-marsh meadow," he is said to have boasted, "and—if there's a black rail nest in it—I'll find it in less than fifteen minutes." In fact the great majority of all black rail nest discoveries were made in coastal New Jersey, in the 1920s and 1930s, the closing decades of the egg-collecting era. McMullen alone is credited with eighty nests, a staggering total but one you can understand when you realize that virtually all of these New Jersey nests were located in very narrow zones of *Spartina* that flanked the inside edge of barrier beaches, a situation very advantageous to collectors. Ludlam's Beach, Island Beach, Ocean Beach, Seven Mile Beach—these were the favorite places; but they are gone. I stopped at one of them once to have a look, Ocean Beach I think it was, and I can tell you it is not a place to look for rails. Beach cottages and Dairy Queens and thumping discotheques are chock-a-block, cars swarm and horns blare in the heat; and gaudy young girls with tans chew bubble gum and chatter, and parade the streets in colored bunches, like balloons.

So do I look in *Spartina patens,* under mats; or in mixed grasses dead and living, Connecticut style? At once, the fine *Spartina* beckons. It is short and unobstructive and the peaty mud beneath is solidly agreeable to walk upon. Easy going, in other words. And it is softly lovely, open country, almost pleasant, despite the respectable heat and a steady following of mosquitoes. But it is practically nestless. Only one bird, the sharp-tailed sparrow, evinces any interest domestically in pure, picturesque *Spartina patens*— a shame, I feel, considering its friendly delicacy. Such unrecognized potential. The sharp-tails: I find three of their deeply-hidden woven cups during my morning explorations, and nests of nothing more.

Nests become more frequent and more varied when you explore the taller, varied grasses. Cover becomes more complex and more mysterious, more conducive, and nests turn up of redwings and seaside sparrows, and I find an old abandoned nest of a rail, probably a Virginia's. What else lies buried in these grasses deeply, darkly, and unfound? What else, Judge Clark? In a heightened and expectant state I continue my search vigorously to its end, without event.

Less vigorously, I wander around in wetter, muddier marsh where coarse stiff stalks of bulrush grow . . . and Virginia rails prowl. They announce themselves with single strident notes you could describe as shrieks—shrieks with body to them, with sonority, if that is possible. Sometimes, surprised, they flush, staying airborne for ten or twenty yards before losing themselves again in the great engulfing marsh; the trajectory is that of a weakly drop-kicked football. In flight you know them to be Virginias by the long projecting bill, conspicuous on a dark brown bird quite undistinguished otherwise. You would not know, from the sight of the dark inconsequential object flapping away that the bird is actually a handsome one: richly, rustily brown and barred on the flanks with black, and embellished by blue-grey on the cheeks and shiny nail polish-red on the base of the bill.

It is hard to think of rails as handsome birds; the usual dim and fleeting view is of a blunt form drab as mud. But the privileged view finds unsuspected color and beguiling delicacy of design. They are beautiful birds, in their own unbright, understated way; theirs is a beauty of subtlety, of texture, of richness of brown and delicacy of grey, a beauty of modesty and mystery.

Sharp-Tailed Sparrow

So much is familiar about this tidal meadow country. So much of it I've known before, in Connecticut in years past: the rugged look of cordgrass swept up into waves, twisted into cowlicks at the whimsy of the wind; the clean *Spartina* sweetness that reaches you when the wind has died; and the feel of vast distances—sometimes bereft, forlorn, and sometimes soothing. And birds: the wailing meadowlarks and redwings that fly up from nests to circle you and scold; and obstreperous swooping willets; and friendliest, most familiar of all, the mixed societies of sparrows, seaside and sharp-tailed, the many busy sparrows of the grass that animate each acre with their comings and goings and breezy, gasping little songs and heads that pop up to see you coming, and gentle syllables that scold you.

Some things are unfamiliar, like knobby loblolly pines and needlerush and southern temperatures and of course that black rail voice you hear at night. Justly, some components of Connecticut are missing here, at Elliott: like the dark green swirling blackgrass, *Juncus,* that darkens the meadow landscape vaguely, splotchily, like cloud shadows; and the sawtoothed leaves and buttery blooms of silverweed, so vital to the salt-grass June of home . . . the meadow is a monochrome without them. Two birds are missing, too, the king and clapper rails. You'd expect them here on these familiar flats of meadow; you'd expect their big, far-carrying calls; you'd expect to see them parading in the open now and then, these biggest, boldest, most visible of the rails. But they are not here.

King and clapper rails are larger, less striking copies of

Virginias. The king is more or less brown, the clapper more or less grey; otherwise, more or less, they are identical, both sporting the long-billed profile and lateral barring of their smaller Virginia prototype. Kings generally like freshwater marshes, and clappers generally like salt. Generally. If all this sounds a little indefinite, it is because it is: sometimes the two live together in intermediate brackish territory, in estuaries; and sometimes they interbreed, and you see intermediate rails, not really brown or grey, not really king or clapper. (Some scientists consider the two a single species now, in fact.)

Let's try this black rail: a sturdy, steady singer in lush green where last night there was none. I'll wait for hours if I have to. The tape begins its ruse, and I dig in firmly with my boots, ready to endure. I'll wait for hours. I check camera settings, swipe at the gathering mosquito whine, look up and around at the stars, then down . . . there he is! He's five feet from my boot, unobstructed, tentatively poised, and ready to scoot. It happened in a matter of seconds—I'm caught in complete surprise, shamefully unready, unpositioned, and undaring to move or even breathe; soundlessly, steadily, inch by inch I heft the apparatus to eye level, find bird in light . . . he's still there . . . then focus with a twist and reach for the microswitch and, with hammering heart, push—*zip. Zip* . . . sound, but no light. No flash! The shutter tripped and the film saw only darkness. I withhold my howl—the bird is still there. Reframe, refocus, hold breath—*zip* . . . no flash. *Zip* . . . and he runs away.

It is not an ordinary assemblage of equipment that I bring to this unordinary task: nor is it untried. It was designed and redesigned, tested and retested, redesigned and retested and redesigned again, refined and rerefined expressly to photograph a certain small bird in a marsh, close up, at night. The arrangement includes camera and autowinder and tele-macro lens and two heavy, potent flash units, main and fill, and big square diffusing screens to soften them; and a single microswitch to fire it all, and a flashlight to see and focus by, all assembled together upon a frame with struts and shoulder brace to make a single, solid, portable "studio." The contrivance is a little unwieldy, and weighty—it gives you a good workout—but it is mobile, and with it you can follow a rail through the grass and know you have good lighting, always and automatically. Good lighting is soft lighting, and that is what the diffusers are for: nothing photographically is more distressing than the frozen, glassy look of subjects struck by a raw, unsoftened flash.

My first arrangement was not so portable. It involved lights on separate tripods and camera on yet another, in an immobile, studio-like affair that might actually work sometime, should the bird ever appear and linger exactly where you had determined earlier that it should. The bird doesn't, I learned. Other changes were dictated by experience: baffles were placed between the two flash heads and the eyes of the photographer, who himself had learned that temporary blindness far out in an unfamiliar marsh at night can impose a serious inconvenience. Placement of flashes, lighting ratio, degree of diffusion . . . all were tested and altered and retested until each optimum was found. So this final arrangement was arrived at by an evolution and by tests. Scores of tests, requiring hundreds of exposures. Hundreds. And always, the flashes fired. Always.

Speechless, too stupefied to howl or to do the only other instinctual thing, hurl the equipment marshward, I pack up and drive away.

It was the flash-shutter contacts in the camera. They failed the first time they were ever really needed, an impossibly cruel coincidence. No work of chance, this; no, it was the stroke of a celestial saboteur. There can be no other explanation.

A spare camera body works with the system, given a little tinkering; and I'm ready to try again. Not yet with vigor, though.

All the rails, it seems, are out to vex me personally. Even the very first one I ever saw, a clapper rail: it was a rankling character.

Old Lyme, Connecticut, where we spent summers, was a veritable wilderness compared to the antiseptic Boston suburb in which I lived; rope-thick grapevines hung in jungly woods, and there were cliffs to explore and blacksnakes to find sunning, and the threat of copperheads, and quartz and flint chips and arrowheads to find in a soft, erosible riverbank. Ospreys and bald eagles patrolled a wild Connecticut River, a river still as wild then, it was easy to imagine, as it was centuries ago when the night fires of indians flickered along its banks.

My friend John and I had connived in a feverish pursuit of birds. We were in our early teens. After finding and learning about most of the local birds in Massachusetts (which did not take long), the need grew strong for new things to see. We were ready for new territory: we were ready for Old Lyme, and a chance at "southern" birds. Exactly what prismatic southern rarities lurked in the outlands of Connecticut we did not know, but I remember visions of yellow-breasted chats, blue grosbeaks, prothonotary warblers . . . expectations were high.

It was June. That first morning, freed at last from an enforced family breakfast, we lit out like prisoners through an opened gate and hiked up along the bank of the river, regarding with little interest the islands of cattails and the faraway chatter of their many marsh wrens. We then turned inland along crumbling Tantummaheag Road, memorable for its catbriers and old stone walls and pastures abandoned but still open, not yet cedar-crowded. One or two lots were being scraped bare for homes; development was just beginning to chew away at the pastoral scene.

High above the pastures was the first new thing to see, seven wheeling turkey vultures. From the dark of woods came our next discovery, a hooded warbler. We heard it singing, and after chasing through a stiff, resistant understory of shrubs we finally found it, a startling black and yellow-green jewel of a southern bird, luminous in the woodland shade. We wandered into a clearing, then, to find the most unlikely scene. There was an excavated pond, freshly landscaped with orderly shrubs at one end and grassy, natural, and disorderly at the

other. As we approached the edge near the grassy, unim-
proved end, something ran from our feet into the pond with a
splash: a dull grey, birdlike animal big as a chicken. We
watched with our glasses; and with long, obvious bill held upward it paddled dog-like across the pond, disappearing into
grasses at the other side.

It was John, I think, who first decided it was a rail. We
delved desperately into our Peterson guide, speedily narrowing possibilities to the two large rails. Our grey bird *looked*
like a clapper, but we had trouble with the text. Clappers like
salt marshes, we read; the rust-colored king rail is the one
found inland. We were stuck. My instinct at this point was to
try to find the bird again. Leaving John squinting at the book,
I ran back and thrashed several times through the shrubbery
and grass; but it was no use.

We were unprepared for an insult such as this, we
proven sleuths; we had been vexed by a drab, unbirdlike bird,
a craven sneak that had appeared at our feet quite gratuitous-
ly, quite unasked for, only to slip away forever without a name.

A few months later I met the mythic author of the book
that so dependably had taught us during our formative days
of finding birds, and that had so failed us that one June morning by the pond. I stood reverently while Roger Tory Peterson
signed my copy of his field guide, and then I told him about the
bird that looked like a clapper rail and swam across a pond in
a place where only a king rail ought to be.

"Was it grey or brown?," he asked.

"It was grey, but . . ."

"Then it was a clapper, but it shouldn't have been
there."

How casual a response, it seemed to me. Here overtly was a violation of the law, a law of his own, set down in his own book . . . surely he ought to be alarmed. But he wasn't; he was unmoved. Amused, almost.

There is a limit to the time you can spend under a Maryland sun, walking back and forth in the infinite green monotony of salt grass, poking about for a nest that might be there. You can keep at it lucklessly for just so long before interest wanders and sanity wanes. After about three hours, even the most fervent railophile loses heart.

Today's search is restricted to an area of manageable size: two acres, maybe. It is a flat of tangled cordgrass in which calling has been dependable on recent nights, and the wonderful thing is that it is isolated, like an island; the surrounding landscape is recently burned over and covered scantily with short green blades, a situation utterly unsuitable for nests. If a nest lies hidden within a mile of these nocturnal calls, it is within these two tangled acres. Possibility is confined, for once.

Twice I search the area through, probing thoroughly the tousled mixes of dead and living growth that seem such perfect sites for nests. Willets dive and scold, and inch-long blue-black horseflies make unrelenting circles that cannot be ignored. A chat mocks from distant thickets. Net result of search: two nests of seaside sparrow, and one of red-winged blackbird. Black rails don't build nests, I conclude; they bear live young, like certain snakes and fish. Or maybe they divide and multiply like single-celled amoebas—at night, of course.

This Elliott Island marsh is hellish in the light of day. When not overtly hostile, and actually torturing you physically by its various ghastly means—mosquitoes, steam heat, and whizzing, pelting deerflies and horseflies—it is at the very least dispiriting. It is a lonesome, uneventful country of empty distances and empty skies and the endless, pointless, lifeless swaying back and forth of grasses, and little else: errant passing gulls, perhaps, and the wind-carried plaints of meadowlarks . . . little consolation here, I say.

At night, however, it is much a different story. At night the meadow is transformed: you are in a different world, a different universe a billion miles away. Everything—the earth, the sky, the very air around you is so charged, so full of energy that you can almost feel it. Yet it is an unrevealing world. The dark marsh is so suppressed, so still, like a land frozen in a spell, that the grasses themselves, dew-twinkling and tightly sprung, seem knowing and alive: *who knows* what magic might go on, when you turn your head away.

Around you everywhere are crickets . . . crickets thrilling, crickets seething, crickets many as the stars; crickets cheering and unanimous.

Around you too are visual assurances, mere pinpricks but important: the voyaging lights of fireflies, fellow vagrants of the dark; and the high, unfaltering lights of stars; and faraway artificial lights describing highways and the arcs of bridges, reminders of the world you can go back to . . . and cold metal glints of dew on grass; and underneath, deep in the dark, exclusive meadow where starlight does not penetrate,

Black Rail approaching

King Rail
Old Lyme, Connecticut
June, 1975

King Rail at nest

Old Lyme, Connecticut

June, 1975

Clapper Rail

Old Lyme, Connecticut
June, 1974

Virginia Rail at nest

Old Lyme, Connecticut

June, 1977

Sora Rail
Douglas, Manitoba
June, 1987

Black Rail at nest

Elliott Island, Maryland

June, 1985

Black Rail

Elliott Island, Maryland

June, 1985

Yellow Rail

Benson County, North Dakota
June, 1991

unseen but all around you, assuring most of all, are the bright red eyes of birds.

You are in a place that matters, and you belong.

Tonight black rails are calling busily. First try is with the one I contended with last time, the one I *would* have photographed, had fate allowed. I ready my equipment—*first* this time, recalling my unpreparedness before; then I start the tape. There is a jiggling of grassblades and instantly, summoned like a genie, he appears in the open with head held down and eyes fixed beadily ahead. In a fumbling, desperate effort I fire twice before he runs back into cover. He doesn't reappear.

Far out in the marsh another bird is just barely audible, and I slog my way out. He too stops calling once the recording plays: good sign. Five minutes pass. I pull one foot from the muck, to shift position, and at once he growls . . . he's in the open, six feet away. Entranced by the tape, this one remains in view for minutes, oblivious to shutter noise and bright bursts of light. Finally he springs upward, and sputters noisily away.

What is *happening* tonight? Where is the celestial saboteur? Openly, in plain view, right under his starry station, I've photographed not one black rail but two, and without a single mishap. Everything has worked. And these two have been so obliging, so beautifully compliant as to seem untutored, and naive. I feel like there's been a galactic oversight and I'm getting away with something glorious . . . but it's no time now to stop and revel, or gloat over spoils, or intone my thanks; soon enough the spell will end and I need to press on, and make the most of it before it goes.

Down the road is a third singer. This one, too, falls silent once the tape starts up, but ten minutes and more go by and he doesn't show. I stoop to reach for the recorder, and out beside it pops a black rail: he scoots over the grass in spurts, as if yanked along by a string, stopping abruptly near the top of a cordgrass tuft. There he stays, crouched, long enough for three photographs. And then he disappears. I was watching, the moment he went, but I didn't see him go.

At the southern end of the marsh is another rail, a fourth, again beside the road. It's becoming a routine: flip on flash-charging switches, check lens setting, start tape player and set it down. Seconds later he is there, rapping on the speaker screens like a woodpecker. He backs off, climbs several inches up a nearby plant stalk, puffs out his chest feathers and growls, then dives at the machine bill-first, like a dart, striking it hollowly. He walks once around the Panasonic monster, pecking at it several times; finding no opposition he loses interest and disappears. Cooing in the marsh is the reason for his proprietary ire: a female, the only one I've heard.

No photographs this time; it happened much too fast. What a picture he would have made, though, the instant before he dove, with his wings held out, the chest inflated, beak agape, and bright red fire in his eyes.

~ 3 ~

ELLIOTT ISLAND
June, 1985

S*ome nights no black rails show,* some nights many do. So it was last year and so it is this year, too. Tonight every rail, it seems, was eager for battle with the tape: one bird actually arrived in flight, landing behind me with a little splash and continuing the rest of the way on foot. Contentedly, with water in my boots and a camera full of pictures, I plod along the road back toward the car.

Headlights approach, and I'm spotlighted as they round a curve. At two AM, in this paludal hinterland, a lone roadside figure bristling with electronic and photographic gear must present a curious sight, if not one that is alarmingly suspicious. The car stops. "Is everything okay?"

"Everything's fine. Thanks for asking."

Pregnant pause. "It's none of my business, but can I ask a question?"

"I'm photographing birds."

"At *night?*"

Along the Elliott Island Road

In the light of day, the farmlands along the road to Elliott are bright and bleak. There is a resignedness toward death and decay about hot, dry, hardscrabble eastern Maryland; it is a countryside of car-killed dogs and possums and woodchucks sunbaked on the pavement for all to see, and omnipresent vultures circling, and weathered old men and women in doorways, staring, and weedy, unkempt cemeteries. Windowless farmhouse shells are left to rot in plain view, like roadside skulls; vines run up and over them greedily and pull them to the earth. Tree trunks stand blanched in the sun, bone-smooth.

Low over the marsh this morning two military jets are performing their thunderous maneuvers. Asail in the same airspace is a single oblivious turkey vulture, performing his maneuvers; one jet blasts right past him, causing him to rock back and forth a couple of times. Undaunted, unperturbed—unflappable, you might say, he continues his clock-slow circle.

Vultures are ever-present in a Maryland sky, ordinary as gulls over water: like mechanical contrivances, they turn forever in their revolutions, unhurried and impassive. Sometimes you see them standing ahead on seldom-traveled roads in groups, studying the dead. Grotesque, indolent hulks, when you approach they make a slow, pained labor of running and rowing, then stroking deeply to gain the air. Sometimes you see them perched on dead, weathered snags, arranged in scenes of stark and deathly drama . . . especially stark and deathly are they after a rainstorm, when, against a dark, still-menacing sky they sit hugely, with crooked, minatory wings held up to dry.

The marsh today, too, like those farmlands, is hot and bright and bleak. I put in my time, though, covering large blocks systematically, if not thoroughly, with long, lazy paths back and forth just as mindless and automatic as the circlings of vultures in the sky. I think of Judge Clark sometimes with envy. It was not required of him that he walk back and forth indefinitely and idiotically in the sun; discovery for him was sheer blessed luck, sheer serendipity. He wasn't even looking for what he found:

> *. . . on the 6th of June, 1884, I made a trip to "Great Island"—a tract of salt meadow near the mouth of the Connecticut River, on its eastern shore—in search of nests of* Ammodromi *which abound in that locality. During a very successful hunt for them I observed a tuft of green grass carefully woven and interlaced together, too artificially to be the work of nature. "Merely another Finch's nest," I mused, as I carefully parted the green bower overhanging it. But wasn't there an extra and audible beat to my pulse when before my astonished gaze lay three beautiful Little Black Rail's eggs?*

Right at my feet a big bird blasts away, scaring the wits out of me, shattering my reverie and exposing its sunken bowl full of duck down and bright white eggs: a blue-winged teal. Except for the ordinary ones of sharp-tailed sparrows, it is the only nest today.

Tonight the dew-sparkling meadow is still and starlit, eerily inviolate. Needly blades lie weighted and twinkling. To walk in so delicate a creation feels violent, even murderous, but I do it; I tear my way through, bruising and breaking stems five hundred at a time with every rubber-booted step, leaving a slick, dark trail in a still and silver sea. I leave behind an Elysium torn and pock-marked and profaned.

But conscience can be overdone. After all I'm here to revere, not to profane. I find no other pilgrims out here; no crushing abundance of human homage to meadows and the lives of birds; most people don't bother black rails. My trail is but a transitory scar; the meadow will restore itself in a week. And the rails, too, will get along. To wights so quick and tiny what could be less consequential than one person dragging his way across their universe of grass?

Soggy and tired, I'm plumped down in a soggy meadow, sitting, half a mile from an unknown road in the middle of the night, about as by myself as anyone can be. I have my photographs, I've done my job. It's time to relinquish microcosms for a while.

How lucky I am tonight, to be here alone with all of this—the space, the stars, the boundless luxury of grass; how unthinkable the moil and blare and filmy public surfaces of cities . . . how inexplicable the places people live. Here the dew is cool, the grass is opulently soft and silvery; overhead the stars are steady, bright, and pure. Across the water far, far away, safely distant, are the glimmering lights of man.

Mindful of the live black rails that populate the dark, I find it bewildering this morning walking in a sunny marsh in which they seemingly don't exist at all. Black rails are like dreams; in the awake clarity of day you find them gone. Not once in all my slogging daylight hours have I glimpsed anything, ever, that could have been a black rail. You'd think I would surprise one now and then and he would flush or scurry away seen, but no.

Humbling, therefore, is the story about that most unlikely black rail ever seen, the one storm-lost that came toppling down through the branches of a pine tree and landed at the feet of a Mr. Cobb, in 1904, at Milton, Massachusetts, substantially beyond its geographic range. Here I am, *surrounded* by black rails in their rightful home, unable to detect one; and this man, to whom black rails were doubtless the farthest thing from mind and possibility, was *delivered* one down through the boughs of a pine tree to his feet. Mr. Cobb chased after it and caught it alive.

So inextricable, usually, are rails from marshes, like fish from water, that when they turn up elsewhere in the open, as they do sometimes by accident, they are conspicuous and befuddling sights, as out of place as ducks in the desert. Imagine the Virginia rail seen walking on a Cleveland sidewalk at night, not knowing what to do, or the king rail standing on a porch in Iowa, waiting out a snowstorm; imagine a migrant yellow rail in New York City, stranded, or a clapper rail paddling across an estate pond—all these have been seen. Rails have been heard in unnatural places, too, at night: a clapper rail outside an apartment building in Connecticut, on pruned grounds; a black rail on a lawn outside a tent in Florida; a Virginia rail from a Connecticut Amtrak station, across the tracks, in an upland cemetery. . . .

Nest site of Black Rail.

Most bizarre of all, though, most lost, was Mr. Cobb's black rail. No other human being standing under a pine tree will see such a sight again.

One nest today increased my pulse, but only briefly: a meadowlark's.

July

On a breezeless July day a salt marsh is an awful place to be. Steady sweat stings your face and neck, and the persistent prickling of mosquitoes occupies you otherwise. Nest hunting is a task, to say the least. It's a defensive effort. Nests found are the usual ones: several of redwings and seaside and sharp-tailed sparrows, and one of a Virginia rail. It must be that black rail nests are so few, and the territory is so stupendously vast, that one really is looking for a needle in a haystack—or a needle in a landscape full of haystacks. The odds are against you.

Through the hot grass I continue an aimless, uninspired course. Up ahead is a disturbance in the evenness of green, an arranged canopy that signals the presence of a nest: a seaside sparrow's, with four eggs. More aimless wandering. Another canopy, another nest: another seaside sparrow's. . . . No, the eggs are too big. Meadowlark? There are six eggs, too many for a meadowlark. A trick? An illusion? I know better, really; the off-white eggs with their spatterings of brown and burgundy are unmistakable. It's the nest of a black rail.

What now? I don't dare touch the thing. I don't dare look at it too long, or even think about it. Speedily I set a marking stake nearby and walk away.

Nest and eggs of Black Rail

Next morning, thinking of Judge Clark and that half-day he devoted in vain to catching his rail at home upon her eggs, I approach slowly and peer into the nest but can see no eggs, only shadow. I lean down closer . . . out jumps the shadow, and with two quick hops it disappears. The image was only a smudge, but I know what it was. In the nest now is a seventh egg.

What is it like to find the Holy Grail? It is unpeaceful and uncertain. I expected to find it gone this morning, erased by the passage of the night, like fantasy; or picked up and moved away, or savagely destroyed in place. But here it is, untouched and undeniable, tied fast to the growing grass and rooted in the peat. Realization is slow.

It is confounding, too. There is an impulse to continue searching, as if it hadn't happened, and find it all over again, or find another. There is momentum to the routine of many, many days.

Except for worrying and doubting, I don't know what to do but marvel.

Land records: that's what I need to find. I need to find the landowners, and get permission to do photography. Propriety, and all that. I need to do this right. At Vienna, where I stop for gas, a businesslike man who owns the station directs me cheerfully to the county courthouse, at Cambridge. I find it, after a mistaken stop first across the street at the county jail; and I find that it is a Mr. and Mrs. in Alexandria, Virginia, who own the Holy Grail.

The phone rings many times and a raspy, geriatric voice of unclear gender answers. I explain my need.

"What are you saying? What are you saying?"

It is a lady and she is hostile. I try to explain lucidly, with utmost etiquette, but she cannot comprehend and with a nasty nasal "Wait a minute" she hands over the nuisance of me to her husband, who is one degree more agreeable and one degree less deaf. He understands; but he isn't friendly.

"I'll send you a picture, if I get one. . . ." I'll say anything.

"We don't want a picture."

They don't want a picture! Permission, indeed; I'll do it anyway.

"OK, OK, you go ahead," at length he volunteers, acidulously enough to please the wife beside him; "but we don't need a picture."

First, before I photograph, there is another call I need to make. To Hal. It was more or less a promise that I would.

Hal is a fellow black rail devotee, a veteran of many years. I met him late one night last year, at Elliott, on the road. "Guess I know why you're here," he said out his open window, as our cars squeezed past each other. We partied that night, right there on the road; we sat on car hoods and talked, drank beer, and listened to night birds until they grew faint, receded, and gave way to the twittering of barn swallows, first voices of impending dawn. If I ever found my nest, he said, I ought to call him. He himself had looked many, many times, had "turned over every blade of grass," as he put it, where he thought they ought to be. So he knew the odds.

Hal's voice was slow and sonorous, warmly southern. Unfailingly his tone was measured, never stirred: not even the subject of black rails could excite a change in pitch, or hurry the delivery. It could cause silences, though; long, far-off silences nurtured by draws on a cigarette.

He answers the phone. I reintroduce myself, remind him of our meeting, and ask if he can think of any reason that I might be calling. Silence follows, faraway silence, then a reluctant chuckle. "So," he says at length; "they *do* build nests."

For three days I've kept my distance from the nest with unimpeachable restraint. But I've peeked in each morning, to count the eggs, because I want to know when production of them stops and incubation of them starts. I want to know when they will hatch, and I want to be there when they do. I have my photograph of the nest, with two red eyes inside, but to photograph the chicks, too, what a coup *that* would be!

Nobody knows the incubation period of the black rail. A good guess, extrapolated from those of the larger rails, which are known, would put it between thirteen and eighteen days. Less than thirteen would not be possible—would it?— for a "precocial" bird whose young are so developed when hatched that within the hour they are ready to run away.

The last egg has, in fact, been laid. It was laid two days ago, on the twentieth of July. Prediction: hatching will happen between the second and the eighth of August.

There are practical matters: work, for example. I don't have ten or fifteen days to idle away in Maryland waiting for a set of eggs to hatch. But the *opportunity*! Here at a known point will take place events probably never seen before, except by the indifferent eyes of insects and meadow voles; here is a chance to be privy to the most occult of moments in the most occult of lives conceivable. It is a chance unlikely to come again. Perhaps indeed, a return trip could be arranged on August second.

2 August

Evening traffic is stop-and-go for two restive hours before finally I break through the New York–New Jersey megalopolis and continue at highway speed for Maryland. Anticipation grows. What awaits, at the Elliott Island nest? Eggs not yet hatched, or downy chicks the size of bumblebees? Maybe the nest has been torn open by a raccoon, now cloyed with a belly full of eggs; or has been pressed flat by a dune buggy tire. Maybe it has been excised cleanly and completely, right down to the bare mud, by some unscrupulous and canny scientist who caught sight of my marking stake and sniffed an opportunity. . . . Or maybe a photographic pirate has seized the chance. Maybe he's out there right now, tonight, at the very site, shadowy and hunched over like a grim, determined grave robber. The dismal drive south affords plenty of time to worry.

Route 13, that interminable strip of Delaware discount liquors and malls and self-serve gas pumps and car lots festooned with multicolored triangular plastic flags, is now a phantasmagorical succession of minor memories ten days old. I remember Arner's Family Restaurant; unfailingly it conjures up a smiling Arnold Palmer, for the thin reason that it almost spells Arnie's. And the Adult Books places: those matchbox houselike shams so frail-looking it seems the traffic breeze should blow them down. Windowless, unfriendly places, timid about their trade. Defensive. They never dare display a name of ownership; you don't see *Arnie's Adult Books,* or *Del Mar Adult Books;* only *Adult Books* (and *Peep Show Too).* Gun stores, too, are holding their own. *Guns and Goodies*, a memorable one, still flourishes.

And the billboards of course; essential to Delaware highway culture is the billboard. *Pray. It Works.* is a new and timely one. Here—I remember this one—is that looming, god-sized, painted face of Warren Price, mustachioed and smiling, your benevolent Honda dealer ("I never met a deal I couldn't beat"). And *Say it here (301-681-3444)* is an old familiar, too; when billboards have nothing else to sell, they sell themselves.

It is midnight when I turn off the car and walk out through the dew-soaked grass. It's a perfect August night: starry and cool, fizzing with crickets. Fireflies blink and meteors scribe bright, momentary lines across the Milky Way. I find the marking stake and angle my flashlight down. Something's wrong. The area is disturbed . . . the nest can't be seen. No, it's here after all. Inside are empty, open-ended eggshells—the chicks have hatched and left.

Well, they made it. Somewhere, in this world of grass, small, dark birds begin their secret lives.

II

Another Bird,

Another Meadow,

and a

Golden Moon

~ 4 ~

When *you've kept company* with black rails on moonless June nights and photographed them, and found out where they nest; you wonder, then, what else there is to do. What now would pose a challenge? Could there ever be another love affair, another bird?

Possibly: the yellow rail. It is an equal miracle of stealth and secrecy, if any creature is.

It is larger than the sparrow-sized black rail, about the size of a bluebird with the tail cut short; and it is slower moving. But this rail is no less a genius of invisibility. It is a masterpiece of camouflage, for one thing, a straw-colored bird that lives in straw. And its motion is something magical: here is a bird that threads its way through the grass with the fluency of a snake. The black rail relies on celerity for escape—quick as a blink it can spring away, like a flea; but escape for the yellow rail is something smoother: it just melts away.

Yellow rails belong to the northern prairies. In June, when black rails are running around in the fine *Spartina* of their southern meadows, yellows are busy in sedge meadows, mainly from Michigan west to North Dakota, northward all the way to Hudson Bay. Of course they don't live in just any sedge meadows; plant species, successional stage, water depth—all must be just right. Snails are a factor too; it is a matter of diet. No snails, no rails.

When all factors are right, though, there is still no guarantee of yellow rails; some sites that seem quite perfect are quite devoid of them. So it is, with birds of personality.

Yellow rails, like blacks, are found by sound, and only very, very rarely are they found by other means. You hear them at night, on their nesting grounds, in June and, to a lesser extent, in May and July. The call is nothing more than clicks: mechanical, typewriter-like clicks not plausibly the work of any bird. "Notes" would seem a flattering word, but notes they are, toneless notes fired off in stutters of two then three: *tick-tick, tick-tick-tick; tick-tick, tick-tick-tick;* and so on, delivered with the driven, disciplined intensity of a machine.

When you read about the yellow rail you read inevitably about a certain place, and a certain man. You read about a place called the "Big Coulee" in Benson County, North Dakota, where yellow rails once lived; and you read about Reverend Peabody, the man who used to find them there.

Reverend P.B. Peabody. Indeed, if ever a man was intoxicated by the magic of a place, and by the magic of a bird that lived there, it was he:

Mr. Peabody is undoubtedly the highest, as he is almost the exclusive authority upon the nesting habits of the Yellow Rail. His unexampled devotion to the quest of this rare and elusive species is one of the outstanding romances of oology. He is good for twenty years more of it; and if ever his spirit is permitted to return, some decades hence, it will undoubtedly be to haunt the marshes of North Dakota in Yellow Rail time.

So it was, with this extraordinary eulogy, in the pages of an obscure journal[*] in 1922, that colleague William Leon Dawson prefaced an article by Mr. Peabody, *Haunts and Breeding Habits of the Yellow Rail,* twelve pages of poetic prose that endures to this day as *the* classic tribute to the yellow rail, and as one of the most evocative pieces ever written about a bird.

In June, 1899, a young oologist named Fred Maltby was exploring the region of this "Big Coulee," trudging through marshes, when he discovered two mysterious nests by stepping on them. Two of the eggs were spared and survived uncrushed, and he sent them to his mentor, Mr. Peabody, for identification. The thunderbolt that struck when the senior oologist unpacked them can only be imagined: at the time, only a single set of eggs of the yellow rail was known to science; and that was an incomplete one, collected thirty-six years earlier in "extreme northwestern Illinois" and kept with scant details at the Smithsonian Institution.

To be sure, Reverend Peabody was stirred by these discoveries, so stirred that two years later, in 1901, he set out to

[*]*Journal of the Museum of Comparative Oology,* 1922, Vol. II: pp. 33–44.

find the "Big Coulee" for himself. And to be sure, he was stirred by what he found. During the quarter-century that followed he was to make more than a dozen of these pilgrimages to North Dakota, all the way from his home in Kansas, to spend June with yellow rails. In 1922, remembering, he wrote about finding the "Big Coulee" for the first time:

> *In early June of a following year, 1901, I made my way across the unlinked area of rolling upland prairie, precipitous ravine, and venerable butte, which lies to the west of Devil's Lake. My destination reached, I hastened across some acres of "hog-wallow"; on over still wider areas of virgin prairie, whereon disported and sang many a blithesome Longspur; and stood at last atop a great butte, looking down upon that deep-lying sea of sedges, rushes, and grasses, known locally as "The Big Coulee." In and out it wound among the hills.*

> *It was a most animated scene. Out among the cat-tails resounded the weird, not unmusical Ou-gl'-ee-ay-ay-ay-dl of the Yellow-beaded Blackbird. Whilomly outrang the trumpeting call of the Pied-billed Grebe. The rustic pipe of Prairie Marsh Wrens, nesting among the cat-tails, added the cheer of unrhythmic chatter to the prevailing symphony. Soft undertones of other birdsongs enriched the music of the meadows. Here and there appeared bright reaches of water whereon were sailing male Ruddy drakes, their mates the while brooding eggs amid the rushes. . . .*

> *One must give reason why this bed of an ancient river should have been chosen as a summer home by that rarest of inland water-birds, the Yellow Rail. The*

Yellow Rail: "Capped Eggs of 1912"
by P.B. Peabody

*winding coulee, deep-set among the hills, is reached by
steep ravines. These are clothed with partridge-berry,
rose, willow, aspen, and the silver-leafed buffalo-
berry.... On top of the morainic buttes are scattered
granite boulders of varied colors, all enriched by wonderfully varied lichens. Amid all these boulders blos-
somed vetches, cone-flowers, and puccoons, in
glowing tapestries. Here, in this most radiant setting,
was the paradisic home of the Yellow Rails.*

Paradisic indeed. You long to accompany the man, so
infectious is his spirit, his ardor, and so tangible is the scene;
you long to hike over the hills and buttes of the past yourself
and join him in discovering this Eden, this morning meadow
riant and seething with the songs of birds. His antique charm
of language heightens your longing, suffusing the picture that
you see with a pastoral haze of days gone by.

Most of Reverend Peabody's days spent in the "Big
Coulee" were spent in search of nests. He found them there,
too, about one a year on average; about twenty in all; and his
protege Fred Maltby found almost as many.

Like other naturalists of old, Peabody and Maltby found
their nests by the most patient, persistent means: by wandering vast territories with eyes trained fixedly down upon the
grass ahead, yard after yard, hour after hour, with day-long
faith that at some moment, maybe the very next, those treasures sought would lie gleaming in the grass before them,
right before their eyes.

Nest finding, like letter writing, is a forgotten art. A few
nests of the yellow rail have been found since those golden
North Dakota days, in Michigan, Wisconsin, Ontario, and

Manitoba; but most of these were found by accident. An ex-
ception would be the modern case in Michigan, at Seney National Wildlife Refuge, where nests were actually *sought,* and
several found: but they were found the olfactory way, by dogs,
not by keen-eyed naturalists. Using trained dogs to sniff out
your nests is aesthetically bereft, of course; it even seems un-
sporting, when you think of the labors of stalwart Mr.
Peabody. And it is unromantic, too, rather like seeking your
soul mate through a computer dating service. Expedients may
speed the search, but the search counts.

Where would you look for nests of yellow rails today?
In the "Big Coulee," where Reverend Peabody did? I wonder;
and I read on:

> One unusual condition has, I am sure, determined the
> fitness of the "Big Coulee" as a breeding place for the
> Yellow Rail. Far up on the top of a butte, rising out of a
> boggy spring pool, there flows a tiny stream of clear,
> sweet water. Down the slopes the streamlet flows, now
> losing itself to view amid lush grasses, and, again, pour-
> ing itself with noisy babbling over some buried boulder.
>
> Across the reach of narrow, coarse-grass meadow
> it quietly flows among the cowslips and sedges. On-
> ward it meanders into the coulee; here it enlarges by in-
> take; then spreads wideningly and sluggishly into the
> broader expanses. Now there appears a stretch or two
> of clean sand amid the alluvial muck. Onward, at last,
> the stiller waters flow, out into one of the lagoons.
>
> No one element of that wonderful coulee is more
> delightsome than this little stream of clear, cool water.

And right here, throughout many of the years of my ob-
servation, has been the focal point of the nesting of the
Yellow Rail in that famous Coulee. Nowhere else in all
that region, during many years, was the Yellow Rail
ever found.

The picture that he paints is irresistible. I too want to
wander among the rails and look for nests, like Mr. Peabody
did. I want to tear through the same perennial grasses he did,
and wade through waters of that same "delightsome" stream,
and roil silts that have lain undisturbed ever since, perhaps, by
any human feet. I want to find this old meadow.

But what if there is no "Big Coulee" anymore? What if it
has changed, and the yellow rails are gone? No matter then, I
want to find it anyway, for sentimental reasons. There are other places to look for yellow rails: elsewhere in North Dakota,
and in Ontario, and in Manitoba. And in Minnesota, too. . . . I'll
stop there first. But I'll bet the "Big Coulee" is where they are.

~ 5 ~

AITKIN COUNTY, MINNESOTA
June, 1987

Spring *is still grey in Minnesota.* Greenness is thin and un-convincing and the air unscented, unsoftened, not yet winter-thawed; it feels more like April than early June, and one lone spring peeper is peeping still.

One June evening eleven years ago I stood here at Mc-Gregor, Minnesota, alongside Highway 65, acquainting my-self with this illimitable prairie marsh. Standing with me was a wife—a good sport of one, too, who did not quite agree that McGregor, Minnesota was the only possible place to spend vacation . . . but there she was. The drive out was a fond ad-venture—fond for one of us, at least, and at least in memory; in a tired old Toyota we braved together the epic drive, survived together the drear, undiffering monotonies of Ohio, Illinois, and Indiana, and the orange stench of Chicago-Gary, and the rolling green monotony of Wisconsin, finding inspiration only near the very end, north of Minneapolis, as spruce woods and sedges first set in.

We were here, or I was here, for yellow rails. We heard them, too. But I never found a nest, or took a photograph, or even saw a yellow rail—never even caught a glimpse of one, though I walked among them many times, encouraged by their clattering calls, which were all around, sometimes only several yards away.

At McGregor this evening Le Conte's sparrows sing sneezily in the roadside dusk, as they did eleven years ago; sedge wrens sing in sedges, and sedges still stretch wistfully to a distant sky. Some things change, though, in eleven years, and it is a little triste, now standing here alone. Wildness once brimming is now devoid and unconsoling; there is nothing out there for the human soul, only sedges and sky and the simple songs of birds busy with their own lives . . . only memory and prairie and a gaseous eternal sky. It has grown dark. A rail begins to tick.

There is another sound: footsteps on the road. Two men appear; birders from California, here for yellow rails. They've heard the ticking and are eager to slosh out after it. I should be too. It's what I'm here for. I should snap out of it.

We drag our way out a very long way, laboring through

water and robust sedges almost shoulder high, drawing near, at length, to the deceptively distant call; we conspire to surround him and close in, and when we do he flushes: in our lights a dark birdball blurs arcingly away. It seems a colorless success, but the Californians are happy. This is not the marsh I want. No question: water is too deep, plants too rank, and birds too few—only the one, in this prairie marsh big as the sky. McGregor is not the place to be.

I make one more stop tonight, a regrettable one, a few miles west on Highway 210. Moments after I step out to listen a sputtering, misfiring Datsun stops alongside. The occupants are two teenage buddies.

"What the hell you doin'?"

I ask them why they feel they should know.

The pitch of the voice increases: "We had *twelve hundred dollars* worth of air compressors stolen from our shed the other night—*that's* why we wanna know."

I'm not stealing air compressors, I tell them, I'm listening for a bird; and this, of course, elicits predictable jeering. I should have told them I was listening for a *Coturnicops noveboracensis* (scientific name for the yellow rail). I sidle back to the car, and once safely inside I lash them with some language and tear away, seething with indignation. I needed none of this, having driven a thousand miles to escape just such inanity. Air compressors? Why of course, my marker plate must have given the gig away. Of course, I plotted it: I drove all the way from Connecticut expressly to steal used air compressors from two unshaven teenage rustics in a rusty, fender-flapping Datsun halfway across the country.

When you fight with a skunk you smell like one, the

adage goes; and so I guess I'm smelling pretty bad. But how in the world could a person be more innocuous, less provocative, than by standing alongside State Highway 210 at 1:00 AM in Aitkin County, Minnesota, hoping to hear a bird?

In warm, waning afternoon light I reach my next destination, the Waubun marsh in western Minnesota. It is a disappointing vestige of a marsh, a pocket neglected by farmers because it is too wet to plough. I do a little splashing around anyway: sedge wrens and sharp-tailed sparrows are common sounds. A Virginia rail grunts once, but there is no clicking here. Too bad, for this is the traditional stronghold of Minnesota yellow rails, discovered in 1959 and touted for years.

In fact, it is this Waubun marsh that provided yellow rails subjected to a study under the aegis of the University of Minnesota in 1972 and 1973. Wild rails were captured and induced to breed in captivity—in outdoor captivity, that is, in a penned-in portion of natural marsh. During the first year, nearly all the rails died; when the project was continued a second year, mortality was "reduced to nearly 30%."

In another study, in Michigan, undertaken by Ohio State University, radio telemeters were used to track the invisible travels of yellow rails in their breeding marsh. The devices were affixed to captured birds by three different means: by harness, by suture (to skin), and by cyanoacrylate adhesive ("crazy glue," to skin). Facts were learned by this enterprise—such as, for example, that incubating females utilize an average of only .28 hectares of marsh. But again there was a body count: two of the three monitored females died, "probably due to transmitter-induced stress."

Egg collecting, that universal pursuit of turn-of-the-century naturalists practiced by even the most reverential devotee, is denounced as barbarous today; and perhaps it should be. But the technically adroit techniques of contemporary science are no less so, when they kill birds. The objection may seem sentimental, but how clinical, how chill is reasoning that sacrifices wild, rare, living birds to the gain of nothing more inspired than data. At least the naturalist-collectors of old produced some poetry.

I should declare my own perversity concerning "science": I'm unfriendly with the word, and the antiseptic laboratory world of star and cell and instrument and data that I take it to suggest. Credit for this view is partly due the prep school biology class of one Mr. Wolf, a program of rote and inculcation so oppressive, so dull, so lacking in life and oxygen that it ought to have extinguished permanently any young boy's flicker of a love for nature. Hours were divided between equally sterile places, the classroom and the laboratory: one room was for memorization of lists of phyla (Pyrrophyta, Phaeophyta, Rhodophyta, Schizomycophyta; Nematomorpha, Rotatoria, Gastrotrichia—I looked them up, to refresh my memory); the other for the orderly slicing up of frogs supplied pickled and injected with red and blue rubber so you could tell arteries apart from veins.

I don't remember my phyla, but I do remember Mr. Wolf. He was straight and slender, featureless as a candle. He wore glasses of utilitarian design, with big black frames, and his hair was cut to the scalp, military style. He smoked. Sitting at his desk before the class he would pause for long, deep draws and then resume his discourse, issuing not a trace of the smoke inhaled for whole tens of seconds, for whole sentences, until you wondered where it all had gone, and how he could do it, and then it jetted at last from his nose in long twin streams. Smooth and steady streams they were, remarkably so, unaffected utterly by the simultaneous process of his speech. He smiled a lot—too much, I thought, for someone who liked facts so much. One other thing about Mr. Wolf: he never once took his biology class outdoors. Responsively, I flunked.

However attributable, or not, to this jaundicing experience, my distaste for the scientific way of seeing things is definite. I do not really care whether yellow rails or black rails or any other rails, or any other birds, are monogamous or polygamous, polyandrous or polygynous—or misogamous or philogamous, for that matter; I do not care to know the length of tarsus or culmen or retrices or remiges any more than Thoreau cared to know "the length of a hawk's intestine." Black and yellow rails to me are a phenomenon unexplainable by means of facts, indefinable by jargon. Thoreau: "The man of science who is not seeking for expression but for a fact to be expressed merely, studies nature as a dead language." Indulge me; consider the reminiscences of lyric Reverend Peabody and then this, from a contemporary scientific paper:

> High willow density in areas of water regimes suitable for growth of C. lasiocarpa might have no effect on yellow rail density, or high willow density might shade out significant portions of sedge and result in higher evapotranspiration from the marsh, thus decreasing the suitability of the area for C. lasiocarpa.

And now return to Mr. Peabody, for counterpoint of spirit; recall his "Big Coulee," and his "delightsome" stream "now losing itself to view amid lush grasses, and, again, pouring itself with noisy babbling over some buried boulder. Across the reach of narrow coarse-grass meadow it quietly flows among the cowslips. . . . " Reverend Peabody was a naturalist of a kind more common in his day, lamentably, than in our own.

Judge Clark, who discovered Connecticut black rails, was another man of Reverend Peabody's stripe. In addition to their common zest for nest finding the two had a common zest for language, too: both wrote with personality and literary flair, and best of all they wrote with a sense of wonder, a sense of awe, something scant or altogether absent in the arid scientese of ornithology usual today. Both men are long gone and unremembered by the world, but what they said about the birds of their affection scores of years ago . . . what they had to say about mystery in Connecticut River country, and perennial magic in a North Dakota coulee, they said enduringly. In their words, the freshness of discovery abides: in dark, somber corridors of university libraries you find it, on embrittled pages of journals seldom opened. It is there to be found, still infectious and still alive.

Benson County, North Dakota, this morning is breezy and bright green with waving grass. Bobbing in ruffled blue ponds are redheads and shovelers, mallards and coots, pintails and blue-winged teals. These ponds are the "potholes,"

for which North Dakota is renowned. Buffeted black terns do their best to hover; yellow-headed blackbirds cling and sway with the reeds. On wires and fence posts, western meadowlarks and kingbirds are periodic yellow brighteners along the road.

There is some uncertainty about this "Big Coulee" of Reverend Peabody's; he never really says exactly where it is. The Benson County topographical maps are little help, for the name "Big Coulee" is printed broadly, implicating a valley many miles long. But fortunately I have a clue, an allusion young Fred Maltby made in an article he wrote in 1915. He was the one who discovered the North Dakota rails, you will recall:

> In the southwestern part of Benson County, between the town of Esmond and the old Glacial River locally known as the big coulee, are to be found a number of wet, springy or marshy tracts which are connected with the coulee by ravines or gullies.

Locally known as the "Big Coulee," he says . . . near Esmond . . . so I'll drive toward Esmond and ask. I ask at lunch, in a rudimentary little restaurant with chipboard partitions between the booths. The cashier hasn't heard of any "Big Coulee," but she asks John, who is sitting blankly at a booth with coffee. John hasn't either, but he asks someone else . . . the question gets bandied about the whole restaurant by farmers who seem to enjoy having a problem to solve—much to my embarrassment, of course; I didn't mean to put out the whole community. But they do come up with a consensus, and John gives directions.

I'll save it, though. First, there is less important business to investigate: Minnewaukan flats, a nearby site for yellow rails discovered by a keen-eared birder who had been motoring at night, and just happened to be stopped at the roadside for a common natural reason (some birders *always* are attuned). Following nicely explicit directions, I turn off the road and drive in through a break in a barbed wire fence and park, and I head out on foot along a fading path into short-grass prairie that sweeps eastward for miles, all the way to Devil's Lake, a silver glint in the utmost distance. The walk is perplexingly dry underfoot for a long way, such a long way that I wonder about those nicely explicit directions; I wonder if this is indeed the place; but gradually the prairie becomes damp, then soggy, and soon I find I have attracted a gentle following of Wilson's phalaropes, circling and hovering. They are solicitous for their eggs, from which they are constantly being displaced, sometimes almost underfoot—here I practically tiptoe. The prairie abounds with birds: teals in linear cross-country flights, and criss-crossing swallows, skimming; and always the circling phalaropes, lovely, ladylike, dove-gentle birds. Two marbled godwits swoosh past closely overhead, berating; they make long, low approaches like strafing warplanes. Yellowheaded blackbird puffed-up dandies sail slowly just for the show of it, just to flaunt themselves.

Now there is standing water, and I'm splashing along flushing soras. Soon, in water now ankle deep, their heaped-up nests appear, obvious clumps in the wispy oriental artistry of rushes over water. In any other situation acceptable to soras, or to any other rails, searching for nests is an exertion, but here they pop effortlessly into view eight feet away. An easy rail nest? There *is* such a thing, here on the watery prairie slough where a prospecting predator must either swim, or be long-legged as a deer.

Some of these sora nests have the most insubstantial canopies: the few available grassblades are tied over in a sparse, laughable effort to conceal, like a man's attempt to cover his baldness with strings of hair drawn over from the side.

Back in shallower water now, along the edge of a ditchbank not quite uninundated, are two fresh nests of Virginia rails. One bold bird sits tight even as I stand right over it, looking directly down.

The Virginia is the least discriminating of the rails; you find it almost anywhere there is marsh. You find it in tidal Connecticut River cattails, in company with king rails, and in Maryland *Spartina,* with black rails; and in Minnesota sedges with yellow rails, equally at home. You find it here, on the watery North Dakota prairie sloughs, living companionably with soras. You find it where there are no other rails at all, in marshy fringes of ponds or sad grey remnants of marsh near cities, even in suburban marshes no bigger than backyards. The Virginia is the universal rail.

The first rail I ever photographed at its nest, aptly, was a Virginia. One languid morning in July on a Connecticut River cattail island I sat on a stool in a brown cloth blind for two ovenlike hours, peering out over my lens at the empty nest, waiting, while rising tidewater filled my boots and the tubular legs of my tripod, as my poor, patient wife sat waiting in a rowboat, frightened by the lingering underwater presence of a monstrous carp. Eventually the rail appeared in view, creeping nestward through the stalks, and ever so slowly, with one eye upon me as I sat still, it entered the nest and settled down and I got my picture.

A fine place, this Minnewaukan Flats. Chock full of birds. But a stop at night finds no telltale ticking; and that is what I need to hear.

The enchantment of yellow rails was not a bygone thing for Reverend Peabody in 1922, when he wrote his overture to them; of that you are sure, when you read his closing paragraph:

> Pages and pages of this sketch have been voluntarily and ruthlessly slashed in the interests of space. Yet the writer must claim room for vaunting the still unexpressed thrills which have punctuated the Yellow Rail quests, and which have, for over twenty years, availed to keep him young. . . . The quest of Yellow Rails' nests is endlessly fascinating, and I shall never be done, I guess, until the grim reaper puts me into his collecting box.

Fifteen years later, in 1937, the grim reaper came for Reverend Peabody. But the pilgrim did go back again for yellow rails, during those years—three times, for which there is some record, in 1924, 1926, and 1928. Of any further of his exploits in North Dakota, if there were any, nothing is known.

I realize, closing in now on those grounds romanticized so wonderfully by Mr. Peabody, that it is not just the place I expect to see; it is the man, too. In reverie I expect to find him there, to descry him in the shimmering distance, wandering, staff in hand, poking at the grasses; a slender figure he'll be, wearing a hat, alone and in his element, essential to the scene. I'll stride my way out strongly through the sedges, breathlessly, half a mile or more, and take him by the arm.... "Were there other years? What *more* do you have to tell? And will you show me where it was . . . ?"

~ 6 ~

The "Big Coulee" is a serious topographic feature; you know it when you are there. You drive through a gently undulating country of golden rolling hills and sage and suddenly there it is before you, unmistakable, a golden valley deeply cut with a bright green irrigated stripe that wanders down the middle. The highway spans it as if it was a river, which in fact it was millennia ago.

The "Big Coulee": well, here it is, that "deep lying sea of sedges, rushes and grasses" once of a man's romance; right here between two sloping walls a man found sustenance and magic three quarters of a century ago. I regard the sight of it for many minutes, leaning against the car. It is quieter, emptier than I imagined. I descend the slope; cliff swallows pour out from under the roadbridge in a smokey stream, like bats from a cave.

It is no longer there, of course, that dreamy meadow of long ago. The floor of the coulee is merely damp, almost solid, and mown, as barren a place as a playing field except for a central squiggle of a wetland you could throw a ball across. This poor shriveled marsh and its tired stream are the vestiges of what was.

Ridiculous, this pilgrimage of mine to Benson County, North Dakota, and a paradise that used to be; it's meadows of the present I should be looking for, not old abandoned haunts and vapors of days gone by, and ghosts. I'm here for photographs of birds.

Imagine, pinning your hopes upon a place so transitory as a meadow, and a meadow seventeen hundred miles and seventy years away, at that. Imagine, expecting to find it there still waiting, unchanged after all those years. Well, I did. I expected a meadow still magical, still tangled and mysterious and threaded through by thin, clear streams, still full of rails. But I should have known.

What now? Where to? There is no "Big Coulee" any more; not here, not anywhere. The idea of continuing is bleak.

But the one alternative idea, giving up, is even worse. To turn right around and face that interstate monotony again, that three-day-long monotony broken only by the fire-belching hell of Chicago-Gary, and by occasional lesser hells, like Buffalo . . . and to face New England again—leafy, snug, adventureless New England; to arrive home with nothing to show, not even a single photograph; to unpack equipment never used, and film that never left the cooler . . . now that is even worse.

Let's consider the remaining options. There is Churchill, Manitoba, where the crackle of yellow rails is said to be almost ordinary. But there is a serious inconvenience to Churchill: the thousand miles of intervening muskeg. You get there by train. Not a viable second-thought jaunt. James Bay? It's about the same. There are yellow rails in Michigan, on the Upper Peninsula, but they are within the sacrosanct confines of a National Wildlife Refuge, where the unaffiliated photographer could expect no welcome.

There is Richmond Fen, in Ontario, a site thriving as recently as 1976 and worth following up by phone . . . but Bruce Di Labio at Ottawa breaks bad news: none calling this year, and it seems to be abandoned. Holland River marsh, also in Ontario, sounds wonderful:

> This extensive marsh stretches for about fifteen miles in a southwesterly direction from Cook's Bay, Lake Simcoe, and is about a mile across, at its widest point. The marsh was a former arm of the Lake Algonquin.

Sounds like it *was* wonderful, at least in 1939. And now? Alas: "Dried up, no longer productive," says Harry Kerr, at Toronto. Both men were amiably amused by my ambitions with a camera.

The winnowed list leaves two chances only: "wet meadows east of Dunseith, North Dakota," site of suspected breeding in 1976, just last year, according to an entry in *American Birds*; and a marsh near Douglas, Manitoba: "certainly one of the best places for hearing, and with perseverance, for seeing yellow rails," says Richard Brownstein in a 1972 contribution to *Birding*. Both are long shots, mentioned only once in my collection of photocopied articles on yellow rails. But both references are recent; and both places are within reach.

East of Dunseith, North Dakota, Highway 281 sails through a landscape smooth and infinite and soothing as the sea, except in the northern distance where it swoops right up to flank the Turtle Mountains (really hills), which parallel the highway westerly for many miles and define the Canadian border. Manitoba lies beyond. It is a beautiful blue and green June day, playfully breezy. Miles overhead are southbound assembly-line clouds, all roundly uniform, Canada-made and time-released in a broad unending flow across the plains. One must get out and walk a little, on such a day, even if only on a gravel roadside.

Faintly—do I imagine it?—in through the breeze there comes a little song, jingling, wistful, descending like a sigh. Where? Not a bird is to be seen; and no sooner do the notes arrive than they are lost, leaving just the ether, just the breeze.

"Wet meadows east of Dunseith" are just barely wet, I find, wet enough to dampen and muddy the sneakers but not to cool the feet—wet enough for blue-flag iris clusters, but not for yellow rails. It *looks* like a yellow rail place, sedgy and complex, and I can almost feel them here, almost hear them; indeed, during a wetter year the ticking would be real, for this is a creature notoriously finicky about its living place, apt to disappear from a site if it becomes too dry, too wet, too shrubby, too something unapparent.

I hear that little jingling song again. This time, it comes from high overhead. Unaided squinting cannot find him; it takes binoculars and they find him high, impossibly high and

Douglas, Manitoba

still ascending, a brave remote speck of a bird holding his own in the high breezes, intent upon the clouds. He is Sprague's pipit, a plain brown extraordinary spirit of a prairie bird: so aspiring a little bird, and why? With such striving he carries his story to the sky, high as he can from the prosaic plain, expelling it at last among the winds.

Exit the trans-Canada highway at Douglas, Manitoba, descend a gentle hill, wind your way through town past twenty unassuming houses, a grain elevator, and a sagging general store, cross the railway tracks, and a quarter mile later there you are, at Douglas marsh, the view wide open before you. You drive across on a slender penline of a road straight as an interstate for the half mile it takes to find the other side; looking to either side while crossing this soft green gulf, you look for miles.

Two binoculared visitors are here already. The sight of them at the roadside is both encouraging and disappointing. They are oldsters: nonagenarians, at least, all the way from New York (the plate on their Volkswagen says so). It's heartening, the idea of a senior couple adventuring in their own aged little car.

Upon approaching to say hello, I find them tapping stones together timidly, barely audibly, and staring down intently with the serious expectation that a yellow rail will appear in the open on a paved road in the middle of the day. This is pardonable silliness; rails make fools of all of us, to one degree or another, at one time or another; but it is quickly apparent that neither knows a single bird they hear or see. Obviously theirs is a dabbling interest. They are bound for Winnipeg, he explains, where they will take the train to Churchill for lots of "life birds," and yes, they are stopped here on the way for that extra lifelist checkmark next to the bird named yellow rail. Innocuous enough. But they are a particularly uninspired, phlegmatic pair, it turns out. He is a brittle-looking man, meek and seemingly tethered at all times to his shorter, far sturdier wife who does not pretend to be so interested in a bird. She is edgy, not at all patient with the whole thing, and a constant grumbler— about the growing heat, the (very few) mosquitoes, the time spent waiting. He, meanwhile, is much too mindful of her every disgruntlement, flinching visibly at each muttering and turning toward her halfheartedly, in deference. It is a dismal picture of togetherness.

Enough of my own grumbling. After all, their presence here bodes well for yellow rails. The place must have repute. And it is a beautiful place of vast and promising wildness, just begging investigation. I'll settle in and find out about this Douglas marsh—tonight. In the dark I'll know.

~ 7 ~

It *is at Douglas, Manitoba,* that all the yellow rails are. I knew tonight as soon as I opened the car door that something unearthly and spectacular was going on. Upon stepping out I am surrounded by a clamorous event. Fifteen? Twenty-five? To the west, individual calls are indiscernible, so many and so ardent are the tickers; an officeful of fevered typists could not produce a mechanical frenzy this intense. Mechanical? No, the sound is electrostatic, rather, like the crackle of a hundred bug zappers on a gnatty night. The air is still and damp, a little foggy, acoustically perfect. Occasionally the lone voice of some other bird, a sedge wren or sora, makes its way momentarily through the clatter; but there is no question: life here tonight is overwhelmingly Yellow Rail.

For some minutes I stand at the roadside and contemplate this wonder. Of course it is too soon to consider actual photography; I need time to digest all this, time to adjust . . . but I do that very quickly, once I grasp the reality; if I wait for some better time or, indeed, some better place, it could be a long, long wait. It's time to get my feet wet. Now. Where to begin? The marsh is about the size of Rhode Island.

I brake and skid my way down the road embankment and skirmish with some shin-high barbed wire, outwitting it finally with a curse and plunging in to find it an agreeable marsh, easy going and shallow, solid bottomed, a pleasure to wade across. Choosing a single, separable call, I slog out through the dark. For a long time I slog along, seemingly without gaining, for the voice is ever-distant; then quite suddenly I'm upon it. I'm only twenty feet away.

I expected to find a creature black rail-like in behavior, and it is fun to find a freshly different sort of bird. When I play the tape back he continues his calling obliviously, though at perhaps a slightly more anxious pace; and quite unlike his counterpart in Maryland, he continues, even as I approach. Now only ten feet away in stiff old straw he begins retreating, still calling and keeping deftly just ahead of me, quite invisible, though his presence is almost pinpointed by the call, only to materialize with a wingburst that sends him twenty yards away. I spend the whole night chasing after him in this way, trying to learn about these new acquaintances. Glimpsed sometimes is a flaxen form weaving, meandering along; sometimes a nodding dove-like head and black empty eye are close enough to tempt photography, but usually the pressed bird takes flight first, explosively. One case is a surprise—he stops

Yellow Rail

calling instantly when he hears the tape, flies in, lands behind me, and walks right up to my feet, black rail-style.

Manitoba dawn is 4:00 AM.

It is a night of eerie, unearthly calm. So inanimate, so icily still is the seen world that a person can't believe his ears, for what he constantly hears is evidence of life: the percussive syllables of sedge wrens, the shrill, maniacal folly of soras, the wingburst and screech of a terrified escaping snipe almost stepped upon; and the busyness everywhere of yellow rails.

It is a bewildering confrontation; the two senses deny each other. Sight strains for evidence of all this activity, any evidence—a jiggle in the sedges, a dark whisk of wings—but there is none to see. It is a landscape inert as crystal.

Stalking calling yellow rails is not so frightfully difficult, once a methodology has been worked out. The best way is to sneak up until you're twelve feet or so away, then cover the area with your flashlight and resume approaching, slowly, watching for jiggled grass as he retreats. Once he's found, you can follow him with long, slow strides if you keep eyes and flashlight riveted on the intermittent path betrayed sometimes by the moving straw, sometimes by the moving bird. There is no relaxing this fixed stare of yours, no taking your eyes off him to see what you are stepping into, or onto, even for an instant, or he is lost.

Actual photography, however, is a very, very difficult matter. The problem is always one of intervening grass. Grass is this bird's medium, as water is the medium of fish; and they keep submerged.

Winding away through the grass, a yellow rail is a fluent marvel to behold. With nodding little dovelike head he steadily seeks, nudges, pries, insinuates his way through, and the rest of him slenderly follows. Smoothly, flowingly he threads his way through tangles and snarls and clefts, along suggested and imagined pathways through stiff and dry, through new and green, through coarse, through fine; with unvarying agility he worms, mouses, snakes his way along.

It would have been wonderful. He was leaning forward, calling, beak upward-held; there was green and golden grass around, and black of night beyond. Above him, drooping, were silvery leaves of willow. A magical instant, and I got it, I fired. But I forgot something, before I did; I forgot to switch the flashes on. It was an instant the camera never saw, and now forever lost, for the shutter's clank sent the subject hurtling away.

I describe myself uncharitably, out loud, as I walk away from this event. Dare I try another bird tonight, after so bungled an opportunity? Dare I presume to consider such a privilege? For my answer I need look no farther than the tape player on my belt. The tape is gone, ejected into the marsh somewhere behind me, where it will lie forever silent. New rule: tape the damned thing shut. I have a spare in the car, but it's not for use tonight. I get the idea.

Dejectedly, I drag my way back toward the road only to stop short, astonished in my tracks: in my light, stone-still before me at the edge of a black, bubbly pool is a photographic gift, a sora rail. Not a merited gift, I know, but does it matter? Photography is undemanding technically, but I'm worried he'll look glassy-eyed and stiff and wired in place, like a stuffed specimen in a museum display. It's too easy.

Soras are crepuscular birds. Here, along the Douglas, Manitoba roadside at dusk there is much clowning around: they "eek" and splash and patter and chase each other about, shrieking, running in and out of view with streaking speed over watery, slimy surfaces, sometimes with wings rowing overhead, assisting. They are nervous birds, constant flickers of their tails, always cautious, and alert, and hesitant, loath to venture in the open even under cover of dusk—but impelled to try. A sora will tiptoe out from the stalks of his cattail redoubt, look back and forth, then tiptoe farther, stop, look back and forth again, advance again—then stop with a jerk and freeze, as if having made a terrible mistake. With a sharp "eek" he will leap back for the safety of the cattails.

Earlier this evening, from the car, I watched a particularly entertaining sora. He walked along a barbed wire tightrope inches above the water, making his way along with head down low and rump held high, flicking his tail and using wings for balance. He stopped once to pick at something in the slime below, and slipped off. He swam for a few feet, then regained the barbed wire, unperturbed, and continued coolly and surefootedly along, looking for something else to peck at.

In fact all of the larger, commoner rails can be comedians. All of them, including soras, defy their railness now and then and walk out in the open on the mud, in plain sight, conspicuous as chickens in a barnyard; and when they do they are silly looking animals. They don't know how to act in an open world: they creep rigidly along with the most ludicrous, laughable deliberation, like stalking indians, convinced they are invisible. When alarmed they freeze in their tracks and wait—unseen, they think.

Soras are plump, dark, blunt-billed, midsized rails that are quite the vocalists, as rails go; their nasal sweet-and-sour whistles are almost melodious, compared to the guttural grunts and simple iterations of the other kinds.

They live in freshwater marshes, often with Virginias, the two prowling the same cattails and crisscrossing in their travels and sometimes feeding next to one another on muddy margins peaceably, oblivious of their differences, like brothers. Sometimes the two build nests adjacently, but nests of soras are relegated mostly to the wetter, deeper regions of the marsh where Virginias cannot manage. Indeed, if a marsh has soras, then almost surely there are Virginias, too. But the reciprocal does not hold true: soras are often absent altogether from wetlands chock full of Virginias, such as Connecticut River cattail isles, where the latter thrive.

The sora was once an abundant bird, and abundantly therefore it was shot. During fall migrations along the eastern rivers hunters made sport of it, poling their skiffs over the marshes at flood tides and flushing the rails before them, felling them with ease and abandon.

A dubious sport, rail hunting, so easy are the targets with their feeble, spluttery, leg-dangling flight. But accounts of nineteenth-century shooting avarice are many, and staggering. "One hundred rails per man per day," mostly soras, was an average bag on the Delaware River in 1846, and up to one hundred fifty was "not uncommon for an expert marksman . . . on the Connecticut River in olden times, when there was no legal limit to the bag." So wrote Edward Howe Forbush, in 1912. Audubon, in 1840, attested to clapper rail slaughter of equal magnitude at Charleston, South Carolina, in a lavishly dramatic telling: "In a few short hours, hundreds have ceased to breathe the breath of life," he wrote; "hundreds that erstwhile reveled in the joys of careless existence, but which can never behold their beloved marshes again." Possibly, the account is a little too dramatic, as Audubon was wont to be; we read of a "poor thing gasping hard in the agonies of death," and "slaughtered heaps" and "cruel sportsmen" and "their joyous feelings"; maybe it is a little too sentimental, and the truth is a little skewed . . . and maybe not.

Few rails are shot today. The sport is an anachronism, so depleted are the marshes, and the rails; few hunters deem it worth the bother. But it is a sport encouraged anyway, by state agencies that invent such generous legal bag limits that they are not limits at all, really; it is the fewness of the birds themselves that does the limiting. In Connecticut, it amuses (and irks) me to report, the limit for Virginia rails and soras is twenty-five: that's twenty-five each day, in any combination, for every person who hunts, and that's a limit that would be liberal a century ago, in the days of the frontier.

It amuses (and irks) me even more to note the limit for king and clapper rails: ten, per person per day. In all of Connecticut there can't be many more than ten king rails at any time, and at times there may be fewer; yet each of us may

Douglas Marsh

shoot that many, every day. And when it comes to gallinules, which are even rarer in that state, you are allowed to shoot fifteen . . . but there aren't that many there. Ever.

I should say a little about my Manitoba afternoons: I spend them in lazy, meandering search of nests. Actually I hope that discovery does not strike too soon, and cut short these hours of sun and sweet dry prairie air so salutary, so necessary after the rigorous military intensity of the nighttime business that is so unforgiving of the slightest inattention. Photography of escape masters as sly as yellow rails is exhilarating, but not easy. Carefree, mindfree sunny wandering is easy. Besides, I can afford to dally. Triumph is inevitable, only a matter of time, as it was in Maryland with that even tinier, wilier mite, the black rail. I only hope it's not *too* easy.

How peculiar my idea of fun would seem, it strikes me, to those who jet their way to island holidays; how lean these hours of sloshing and slashing through sedges would seem. But I'd not trade them for the most opulent of holidays. Hours spent poolside with tanned, contented people, and nightlife with white jackets, jazz bands and gin would be wasted on me. For what I have here is my own island, my own resort, my own private playground, and it happens to be wide open and wild and free and waving in the breeze. It is a complete place, insofar as a place can be, zesty by day and magical by night.

Down to business now. Time to take this searching seriously. Historically, almost all nests of yellow rails ever found were hidden in, and under, flattened-down dead growth. Descriptions are like these: "beneath a flattened swath of dead rushes" (Gaspé, Québec); "concealed by the previous year's growth of overhanging grass" (North Point, Ontario); "in a dense mass of fallen rushes" (Munuscong Bay, Michigan); in a clump containing "much dead grass, which formed a canopy over the nest" (Bradford, Ontario). Such is the evidence. However, there are exceptions; for instance, those found in the "Big Coulee." Peabody:

> . . . *very few have been found amid masses of dead grass, and most of canopies have given evidence of being made of hay-masses found ready to use. My own nests have all been found in clean land, amid wholly-green grasses.*

So I'm not convinced that dry, dead sedges are the only answer. Rails, of all birds, are the least likely to be bound by rules; nesting sites preferred in one locality might be forsaken altogether in another. Take the black rail: in New Jersey, in the old days, scores of nests were found beneath thick mats of cordgrass *(Spartina patens),* but no amount of searching there will find you one in Maryland. In Maryland you look where the knee-high *Spartina* is loose and mixed with other grasses. I know. And I know better than to rely solely on those accounts of yellow rails nesting under dead growth; here in Manitoba they may do something very different. Better to search in every possible place, and trust to luck. But luck is not bequeathed today. All I can find is the nest of a sedge wren, and one of a sharp-tailed sparrow.

The calls of rails are about as primitive and unmusical as calls of birds can be. Especially so these surrounding ones tonight, these inorganic clicks you can't believe are authored by a bird, or anything else alive; no sounds could be less musical than these. Yet there is excitement to them. There is intensity. You sense that every caller is possessed, he is unstoppable, he is anxious constantly for all the future notes unstated: he is not yet through one volley of his notes, you sense, before he is intent upon the next. He is determined and inexhaustible.

Rails are not the only birds that are musically incapable, of course. In fact many of the so-called "songbirds" are just as unendowed; and songbirds are simple characters that do not have the personality and aura of the rails. When songless they are unendowed indeed, with little to recommend them, unless they happen to be pretty.

Songbirds are the likeliest of birds to be bright and gay, but there is a satisfying justice that prevails: the most brightly colored ones are often vocally the dullest. Take most of the warblers, for example, with their weakly sizzling little songs; and the witless ditties of finches and tanagers and buntings. Sometimes it seems that there is a justice in the natural world—not just cold uncaring randomness and chance but justice, and justice seems to have been a factor in deciding which birds can, and cannot, sing.

A few birds are doubly gifted, like the bobolink—now there is a bird to see *and* hear. But songs of the dreamiest beauty almost always come from the homeliest of living origins: brown ones, usually. Think of the resigned, ethereal evensongs of thrushes, and of wrens, little birds with big songs. Think of the thumb-sized winter wren and that lingering, tinkling music of northern ravines that stops you and holds you still. And certain sparrows: think of the simple field sparrow, and its sad and faithful whistle remembering, and asking why.

What, meanwhile, do we get from rails? We get grunts, mostly, and whinnys and yelps and shrieks; and simple repetitions that befit machines, like the typewriter-ticking here tonight.

Having lost myself for a time in a fine chase after golden birds and photographs, I return to the road and walk along in a thrall, wishing that night would not end. Yellow rails have all but silenced now, their fervor spent; the fantastic clatter of the first dark hour is reduced to short, sporadic afterthoughts in distant places. It is a peaceful night. Or *was*. Now what is *that*? Ahead, in the deep arterial stream where it flows under the road are splashes, thunderous splashes, and I can't imagine what's making them—big plunging animals, I suppose, unless someone hidden is dropping cannonballs. At my approach the fun stops . . . the water is motionless, evincing not a ripple, not a clue. It must be the nonsense of disporting beavers. Behind me now is a new sound, more ominous; the baritone of a decelerating V-8, which rumbles past and stops.

Very alone and very late at night, in the company of creatures more innocent than those that drive cars, it is a time to bask in simple good feeling, to feel contented under the stars, and belonging, and grateful for the whole glittering scheme. I do. But this is a fragile spell that can be broken by so little as a car. It is as if a switch were flipped: at once the gleaming heavens recede and dim and I alert galvanically, with a good strong jolt of caution. I don't trust my human fellows— these fellows, at least.

Is it *too* strong, the jolt of caution? Imagination can be vulnerable and wild, so late at night.

But there are two of them, probably bold with drink, and out here they could kill me just for fun and stuff me into roadside mud and get clean away. Survival plan: a full-power blinding, point blank Sunpak blast of the flashes into wide-open, unsuspecting eyes. Then a quick drubbing of skulls— two weighty blows apiece with the capacitor butts should do it; I'd have only to stride back to my car and drive, leaving them staggering insensibly in circles, moaning, clutching heads, collapsing.

Maybe it won't be necessary. I compose myself. With contrived aloofness I walk past the driver's window, whistling.

"Do you want a *ride*?" he asks. The passenger-conspirator beside him is tittering.

"Oh, no, but *nice of you to ask. . . .* " my politeness befuddles him, I think. He's struck silent for the moment. Then clutch pops and tires howl and the car makes a slow smoking path away, fishtailing absurdly. I feel that I won the encounter. But it's been an unpeaceful week, contending with these automotive yahoos.

Automotive yahoos are not individuals but always pairs or groups, organisms reliant upon multiple parts for the courage to do their mischief. The individuals themselves are flaccid, formless characters incapable of opinion or confrontation. If I were to meet any one of them in squarely even circumstances while going about my business, face to face and eye to eye, he would dare say not a thing, except maybe "hi."

Sour encounters at night are not the rule, really; nor is this theme of mine unvaryingly a misanthropic one. Usually, if someone stops it is out of simple curiosity, or a concern that you might need help. Warmly memorable is a Maryland couple, both schoolteachers, I think, who asked twenty minutes worth of questions and listened spellbound when I told them about the secret little black rail bird that creeps in the marsh and calls so late at night. Thereafter, when driving past they would wave eagerly from the car, once with the added shout, "It's good to have you *here*."

It's been a fine night for photography—fine for consuming film, at least; I've used up two full rolls. But I made a mistake tonight: I slogged and slashed my way across the entire span of marsh from one side of the valley to the other, fully weighted down with camera outfit, an exertion I wouldn't repeat for any photograph. Midway, I found myself in a no-man's-land of waist-deep water and tall, smothering sedges, but I kept going; I kept thinking I was getting through the worst of it, but the sedges kept getting taller, the water deeper,

until, exhausted, I actually considered turning back, a desperate and awful prospect which would have meant repetition of
all the punishment endured so far, something I wasn't sure I
would survive. I did keep forging ahead, and went the
distance . . . and survived, I think.

Enhancing the unpleasantness of the ordeal, I admit,
was the ineradicable notion that at any one moment I might
slide down and out of sight forever. It was a notion instilled by
a little incident at dusk, two nights ago. I was wading around
in watery roadside slop, trying to photograph soras, when a
military jeep strained to a stop and an authoritative bellow ordered me to get out.

"Don't you know there's *quicksand* out there?"

Feeling reprimanded, like a child caught doing something wrong, I almost laughed, but I caught myself; for he was
very serious. Speechless, I just stood there knee-deep, until
with a stern forward jerk of the jeep he left, his duty done.

Quicksand. Then there was the red-headed fellow at the
general store this afternoon who talked affably about two
cows he had lost out there on the marsh somewhere, presumably to the same malignant downward-sucking forces. And
this, in turn, recalls an experience I had years ago after striding blithely through a marsh. It was in Cromwell, Connecticut,
at a place called Dead Man's Swamp, not really a dangerous
place, as the ominous name suggests; or so I thought. I
floundered ashore after a strenuous adventure and was met
by a man, a hunter, who wanted to talk about the "springs" . . .
look out for them, he warned. Eagerly, with animated eyes, he
recounted the time he misstepped and found himself suddenly
cold and in the dark, submerged, unable even with the tip of

his rifle to find the surface. Obviously, he had managed to bob back up again.

In any anecdote involving muddy, miasmatic places like swamps and bogs and marshes you can expect hyperbole, and an element of superstition. But how do you know when there might be truth you ought to heed? I basically believe the hunter's story about the "springs," I think, though it might have been embellished just a little; but about the perils of Manitoba "quicksand" I'm much more skeptical. Cows, yes, could wander stupidly and heavily into unvegetated mire and sink; but could a person, even if he tried? The notion that quicksand can suck a person downward is certainly a silly one, useful though it is dramatically in television westerns and in literary works like *The Hound of the Baskervilles*, the Sherlock Holmes episode, by Arthur Conan Doyle, in which the hideous "great Grimpen Mire," that no-man's–land of "green-scummed pits and foul quagmire," evokes more evil than the villain.

Springs? Quicksand? They are ideas that prey upon you easily, when you are struggling through unknown regions in the dark half a mile from solid ground in a Manitoba marsh. At any other time, though, at any other time at all, I believe that anywhere, in any sort of marsh, where live vegetation has taken hold it is safe to step upon it. So far, for me, the tenet has proved safe.

Marshes are not such vile places, really. Reasonable people avoid them, it may be true; but if they do it is only because they are unpleasant, and inconvenient, and there is no good reason to muck about in them. Life is unpleasant and inconvenient enough. Even when there are good reasons, like rare birds, marshes seldom are beloved places; even the most fanatical birdwatcher who jets his way across the country, or hitchhikes, or tootles by Volkswagen, even he thinks twice before stepping out in the uncertain marsh, clattering though it may be with the yellow rails he has come hundreds of miles to see. When he does venture out it is with hesitancy, and once satisfied with his glimpse by flashlight he makes his way back directly to the terra firma of the road.

Some marshes are nasty places. Never really treacherous maybe, but surely nasty. Dead Man's Swamp in Connecticut is such a marsh. Tall, tough interleaving sedge blades impede your passage and lacerate your hands, if you part them too assertively; and with every labored step you sink gurglingly into what would be only lake water, were it not for the mass of living sedge that temporarily bears your weight. You either keep moving or sink, and to keep moving in this jungle lushness requires the sort of exertion that on a hot, humid day might kill you. Add insects to the regime, and the misery is thorough.

Some marshes, on the other hand, are truly pleasant places. And some fall in between these two extremes: this Douglas marsh, for instance, with its moderate density and water depth and variously gentle, kindly regions and arduous ones as well, such as that awful one traversed tonight. And the pleasant marshes? Most pampering of all are those aromatic tracts of fine, soft *Spartina patens*, yellow-green grass of the salt meadow, like those at Elliott Island, Maryland. Solid and peaty, merely damp, these are easy to wander as a golf course, or the village green. Few places can be so pleasant as a sweet breezy landscape of June *Spartina*.

When you have found a bird's nest, you have found him out. You have found the very center of his life, and his dearest secret. In the case of small, ground-nesting birds especially, the difference between secrecy and discovery is the difference between success and failure, life and death, continuance and oblivion; and the nest is always many times harder to find than the bird itself. It has to be; no egg ever ran, or flew, to escape a predator. Think of it: during its first days a bird spends life as a bite-sized, encapsulated lump, a vulnerable lump indeed, defenseless as a candy on a plate. Small wonder that birds hide their nests with every last evolved instinctual whit of cunning that they have.

Small wonder, too, that this searching takes a long, long time, for I'm contending with a creature plenty cunning. The days pass rewardless, one after another; inevitably, the search becomes a chore. Except for the legs, which perform their steady task automatically, it is the eyes that do all the work, and they, too, take to working by themselves, constantly processing the view before the feet, ever scanning for that slightest incongruity worth signaling to the mind. The mind, meanwhile, is free to think of other things, or nothing much at all.

What *does* go through your mind, while the rest of you is functioning in this automated way? Sometimes you think about the Great Moment of Discovery. You wonder when it will happen and where, exactly where. Will it be in a place watery and lush, freshly green, with tall bent blades overhanging? Or at the meadow edge, where concealment is brittle, dead and dry? Ensconced rightly in just what perfect setting will be those off-white treasures, eight or nine of them, with their large-end wreaths of spattered burgundy? And when you are allowed the sight at last, you wonder, how will you respond? With whoops and hollers and leaps for joy? Dazed speechlessness? Or solemnity, and mutterings of thanks? Dazed and speechless was my state when the Moment of Discovery struck in Maryland.

You wonder just how the accident will happen. You run through scenarios, and practice reminiscences for posterity: "There I was, resigned to defeat, about to turn around . . . " or, "What possessed me to check that one unlikely clump, I do not know." You wonder too just how many moments you've missed because your path veered a few feet too far this way, or that.

You think sometimes of all the people busy working in the world, people building roads and growing food, demonstrating toasters, teaching children French; you think of men and women confined to stations, to sales counters and desks with phones, and trade-show booths; to drafting boards and lathes, and cash registers, politely ringing totals. People are contributing, producing . . . and meanwhile here you are, far from it all, unaccountable and free and frittering your time away: the rest of the world is profitably, industriously engaged and here you are looking for the nest of a bird, and not even finding it. Or you think about a face at home, or years gone by, or your small black dog, now gone, and how he would have loved these breezes and meadow scents, how he would have run eagerly around in zigzag exploration, nose first, with tail curled stiffly up like a question mark above his back. Or you think about your visit earlier this morning to the library at the university, and the woman who helped you there, the one at the reference desk, fiftyish but comely, well-kept, whose magenta lipstick matched perfectly the magenta of her blouse. Or, desiccated, you think about thirst. Sometimes nothing matters—not love nor memory nor even yellow rails—nothing matters at all except a remembered service station, fifty cents, and a soda machine that works.

It is an endless stretch of sameness, this sedge country, a featureless scheme of living green and sere dead straw unvarying acre after acre, hour after hour. Knee-high sedgeball nests of sedge wrens punctuate the search, but even they become predictable and just another ordinary element in a landscape without surprise. Very occasionally, as if meted out to provide just enough novelty to keep the search alive, nests turn up of various other nesters in the marsh: Le Conte's and sharp-tailed sparrows, and blue-winged teals, and snipe, all nesters except, of course, the target one.

Photography has been blessed tonight. After long pursuit into a far corner of the meadow through fleshy young grass and cowslip leaves, one closely pressed, conciliatory creature stopped in the open on a tussock and crouched and called, and he did the same again and again, as if to ensure that I would get it right. I did, I think; but if I did not then I, not

Providence, am eternally to blame. With so slippery a subject in so dense a medium, one could hardly hope for better.

Am I done, then? Am I content to pack up and go away gracefully, glad for what I have? Not me; too fundamental is my photographic greed. I want more. Manitoba night is a reservoir still full of possibility: photographs of unknown forms still swim in the dark out there like shapeless fish in an enchanted pool. I want more. I want them all.

I went to a library today, at Brandon, to look for articles on yellow rails I hadn't read, and I found a few. One of them is interesting. In light of all my futile hours spent scouring the sedges for nests you can imagine my surprise, and the strain to my sense of humor, to read about the man who wandered out in an Ontario marsh at night and flushed a yellow rail almost underfoot and found its nest with a flashlight. The man's name is Ian Jones, and I hope that he, too, knows that life is unfair. He wrote about it in *The Shrike*, the bulletin of the Ottawa Field-Naturalist club:

> . . . *as I was walking cautiously with a light held before me, a second bird took flight from within 20 cm of my foot. As it fluttered hesitatingly away I knelt down and, moving a dense layer of fallen dried grasses aside, uncovered the nest from which the bird had flown. The nest was loosely constructed of grasses and appeared to be suspended 10-12 cm above the water saturated "ground." The nest contained six brown-spotted, oval, cream-colored eggs.*

Luck, the blessing and the curse.

It is a sober moment. I stand at the Manitoba roadside listlessly, this afternoon, while a mute, compliant prairie surges and falls and rolls with the wind resignedly, and endlessly, like the surface of a sea. It is clear that this search for nests has all but ended, and failed. There's nothing philosophical to say; it's just that my ambition has ebbed away. You can endure the company of sedges, only sedges, for just so long. Austerity has won. But I make the effort one last time. I drag my way out in the marsh and make a final ritualistic loop around, expecting and finding nothing.

It is another of those eerie, unearthly Manitoba nights. Afloat upon the meadow is a golden moon, fully round and glowing; arcing blades of sedge are silvery and still. The whole surrounding world is vaporous, and luminous, ethereal as a movie in a theater but three-dimensional—holographic, actually. It *looks* real; it looks like a landscape made of moon and sky and sedge and faraway wispy willows, but I don't think it is. I think it is only dye and dust and mist, suspended. There is no hardness, no sharpness of edge, no distinctness I can focus on, try as I may. And nothing changes, nothing moves. It is a spellbound scene, a dream held still forever: nothing in the world will ever be again, except this meadow darkness almost green, and silver dusty haze, and thinning gold of moon.

One last time I duck in under the neckstrap and heft my assembled weaponry, and wade out among the clattering rails. I'm fussier now about these photographs, having finally

satisfied my shutterlust, and having garnered quite a tidy
booty, really; I must have a hundred images by now, all wound
up safely in their canisters and sealed and cached in the motel
room under lock and key, in a suitcase among socks, like stolen
gold. There is no *need* for photographs, when you have securi-
ty like this; so I work leisurely, firing only when especially inspired.

What a sight I must be, against this moonlit sky to a
crouched rail looking upward through the latticework of
sedges. What do they make of the monster looming over them,
the sky-god monster with its single staring flashlight eye and
strange appendages that hiss and whine and lash out willfully,
furiously with their electronic flash of lighting? What *could*
they make of it? I wonder.

I wonder too about those rails I failed to photograph,
failed to even find, the female ones. They're out here, all right;
silently, alertly, across these miles of meadow in places never
to be seen they sit in straw-built nests under straw screens,
unsilvered by the foggy light of moon. How many? Where? I
can only wonder. Everywhere, meanwhile, insistently in evidence are the males: everywhere with unstoppable momentum they sustain their din as doubtless they have for uncounted
nights, and for uncounted Junes here in this sedge valley once
a river, under this moon. The yellow rails sing steadily, stead-
fastly, timelessly beneath the rising golden moon.

III

Going Back

~ 8 ~

NEAR TORONTO, ONTARIO
June, 1991

To one accustomed to brusqueness, *as anyone is who lives in the northeastern United States, Canada is always a nice surprise. Even as a motorist, traveling in your capsule, you can't help but enjoy the difference; it's there whenever you stop the car. Attendants at gas stations actually look at you, engage you, give directions cheerfully, and call you *sir*. It is a little suspect, at first. This boy at the Petro Canada, for instance, quite occupied already, piercing a can of oil for one car while another is taking gas: why would he take time to walk me to the street, point down to a certain stoplight, and linger there politely while I make a sketch of his directions? What does he want from me?

I find this same kindliness again, at the very next stop I make, however. Lost again, thwarted in my effort to follow Route 12 north because it has been broken up by highways newer than my road atlas, I pull in behind a convenience store, where a young man is unloading a truck. He is a lean young man, strong, but with a gentle face. "Excuse me . . ." He puts down his case of soda cans, and walks up to the car. He stands there, listening, able arms idle at his side. He looks at my map, then at me, back and forth, with concern on his face, and spells out directions slowly while I jot them down. This patience, this sensitivity, is unaccustomed luxury and I thank him strongly, maybe overdoing it a little.

"Gosh, no trouble 'tall," he says. "My pleasure, sir. I hope that you enjoy your trip." He watches as I go, and waves goodbye.

Here again this morning, when I stop for gas. She is an unlikely source of cheer, this lady immured for the day in a glass cube, with only a cash register and maps and gum and candy, but she is bright, well-wishing, full of smiles. I would be wan, and surly.

Far north of Canadian humanity, which crowds itself along the southern border, the north woods flanking Lake Superior are so empty and so still that you find yourself uneasy, if you are alone. You are so alone, so alien.

It is a coarse country, coarse and primitive, a black, jagged dagger-landscape of spruces massed and poised upon the hills, hostile, like the lances of a mute and ready army. It is endless, this alien country, and it is monotonous. There is no relief, no life, no color. Mile after mile all you see is spruce and sky and black patrolling ravens, mock birds, mere simu-

lacrums of things alive. That's all. You stop and roll your window down to listen. A few thin songs of warblers manage in
the northern air, and a white-throated sparrow tries out his icy
whistle; otherwise, the stillness is perfect. The land is ancient,
frozen hard, unthawed since glaciation you might think. After
an hour or two on this cold planet, you begin to wish for a
world more animated and more evolved, more mysterious—
the night world of a Manitoba meadow, for example.

The better route to Douglas, Manitoba, and that meadow, and that golden moon, is from the south, via North Dakota and the Turtle Mountains. That way, Manitoba greets you
with drama; you descend through aspens to a wondrous gold-
en plain. This way, arriving from the east, you are greeted
rudely. Eastern Manitoba is a dry, discouraging country of
trashy copses and slashings and fallow fields, a messy patch-
work—or a jumble, rather, a northern nowhere-land neither
forest nor plain, neither east nor west. But the road is smooth
and true, and gradually things improve; by the time you reach
Winnipeg you are on the plains, and they are golden.

It is unsettling to make the turn off Trans-Canada 1 and
to descend the little hill again to Douglas. That dark marsh, and
that golden moon: they live indelibly, from afar; but now, this
close, they are imperiled. The memory is no longer safe, when
you go back. It might dissolve.

The sagging general store is gone. Erased completely.
The grain elevator, too. It rose right here at the railway cross-

Sedge Wren

ing and towered above the town, a landmark you could see for miles. In the evening, as you drove out to the marsh from Brandon, the last light of sunset dying in the west behind you, one firelit windowpane burned bravely in the blue-grey sky ahead like the beacon of a lighthouse, heralding your destination. No more.

Otherwise, Douglas is intact. And it is all asleep tonight, except for one roving dog.

The marsh, to my great relief, is still here, still hazy and forgotten. Even the cool Canadian smell of it is just the same; I step out of the car and breathe it well. Sedge wrens are chipping, dozens of them. But the rails? There are only two or three, and their calls are distant, tentative. There is a moon, but it is cloudy-white, not golden.

No matter. It's fun to step back in and wander after other, unrail-like things, like sedge wrens, and photograph them clenching sedge stems, singing with their mandibles spread wide. Buzzing in shrubs at upland edges are Le Conte's sparrows, but they are wary characters; they disappear before you can get quite close enough.

Here is a startling sight: three human figures planted knee-deep in the grass, still as the shrubs I mistook them for. The van . . . of course; I had forgotten. There was a van parked down the road when I left the car, a brand new space-age model, top-heavy as a bus; and it was listing, veritably teetering on the gravel roadside. I think with two fingers I could have tipped it over and down the embankment and into the marsh upon its bubble roof.

Perhaps I should have. My first instincts are welcoming ones, at the sight of these three men; I think I know why they are here, and a prompt burst of clicking near them confirms that indeed I do. We are kindred spirits, we four; we are a freemasonry. I walk up with confidence, but it is with stony silence that they greet me.

"Hello," I venture to communicate.

There is a pause, then a reluctant mumble from the fellow nearest me: "Hello." And then more silence. The secrecy, the *stinginess*, is palpable.

"Having any luck?" I try again.

"Oh, not much," he answers casually, with hands in pockets, almost smiling, trying to seem idle, like he's waiting for a bus. He quite ignores, or pretends to ignore, the resumed clacking of the rail, obviously hoping that either I cannot hear it (how could I not?) or I don't know what it is, and do not care. But all the bizarre equipment I'm wearing is something he can't ignore, can't even pretend to. "What is it you're trying to photograph?," he asks.

It is a hostile question; "trying" is the only word he gave some stress to. Now I feel stingy. "Oh, well, the rails, and other things," I say reluctantly.

Wise now to my awareness of the rails, he makes it clear that this one, right here (it is silent now) belongs to them. "We've chased it for two hours," he says, with a chuckle intended to belie the adversarial nature of his position; "We're going to stick with it until we see it." In other words, get lost.

Some freemasonry. I didn't want to steal their rail, or scare it off; I only thought they'd like to talk a little. Why, for all they knew I could have helped. I'd do as well at a convention of stockbrokers, or realtors, or Kawasaki dealers, in my search for kindredness of spirit.

Well, good luck then, I wish him, and he thanks me with equal insincerity; and without any further ceremony I trudge off in the direction of another rail that has started up, a couple of hundred yards away. I concern myself with him, readying the camera and flashes, flipping switches, sneaking up. . . .

"Hey!" It's my friend again. He's bounding toward me through the marsh. "Hey, man, don't flush that bird!" The roar of his voice is muffled when it reaches me, absorbed by the intervening grass.

"You want *this* bird now?" I fire back forcefully, in rising anger.

Closer, he calms, explains. "We're going to try the one back there for ten more minutes," he says, "then if we strike out we'll try this one over here, and if we strike out again we'll give it up and move on."

Why this territoriality? All they want to do is see a bird, and put it on a list—collect it, as a philatelist would a stamp, and then forget about it. For a moment I ponder the prospect of snarling back, asserting rights, taking a manly stand; then I cover up the camera and walk away to find another rail very, very far away.

Pertinacity looks commendable, in retrospect, when it ultimately gets results; otherwise it just looks foolish. Foolishly once again I've frittered away whole afternoons in this Douglas marsh, three of them this time, and I haven't gained one flicker of insight into the nesting strategy of these phantom

birds. It's perfectly remarkable, that I could sustain such perfect failure for so long a time; it would seem against the odds.
The rails are out to vex me. Still. However, there is a certain
distinction I can claim; I've now spent more time looking for
the nest of a yellow rail than any other man who failed to find
one. And more than most men who succeeded, I might add.
Indeed, in all the recorded history of ornithology there are only
three who have searched more doggedly and more devotedly
than this unlucky pilgrim has: Mr. Peabody and Mr. Maltby,
the pioneers, who spent so many Junes in North Dakota, and
found so many nests; and one other man, Carl Richter, who
found a number later in Wisconsin, over a period of years.

Others less dedicated have found nests too, sometimes
with demoralizing ease: like L.M.C.I. Terrill, who found one
ten minutes into his fifth short search in a little marsh at
Gaspé, Québec, in July, 1940. And John Lane, who found several in some little marshes he called "buffalo wallows" right
here in Manitoba, near Brandon in 1962. He found his first
nest just *one hour* after he began to look, for goodness sake;
how rankling a thing to read! Truly I am the unluckiest galoot
to ever set foot in a marsh full of yellow rails. Among the others who found nests, without expending Herculean efforts:
Harry Heaton, who found four nests in one year, 1939, in
Mono County, California; J.B. Dixon, who found seven there
between 1949 and 1954; and R.D. Elliott and R.I. G. Morrison,
who found a single nest at North Point, Ontario, in 1976. The
list undoubtedly goes on.

Last, and they cannot be overlooked, are those most demoralizing characters of all who simply lucked upon their
nests, just happened on them, like that fellow in Ontario, Ian

Jones, who almost stepped on one at night and flushed the bird from it, with galling good fortune; and Otto Devitt, also of Ontario, who did the same, except that he flushed the bird in daylight, and it was after some earnest searching. This was back in 1917; and his was the first nest for Ontario—the very first for Canada, in fact. California's first nest, too, was found by accident. William Leon Dawson and two young assistants were exploring a marsh at Long Valley on the sixth of June, 1921:

> We were dragging a rather thin stretch of marsh grass when a Jack Snipe flushed and I called Stevens to my assistance, leaving Bobby, who was more remote, standing listlessly by his rope-end. Returning from a fruitless quest, we were about to resume operations when Bobby exclaimed "Well, look at this!" He had been standing all the while within three feet of a low-lying cushion which held, in a compact and perfect circle, eight fresh eggs.
>
> I considered the exhibit long and carefully, too sobered, for once, to render snap-judgment. The boys became impatient and pressed for an expression of opinion. Finally, I said "Well, boys, to the best of my knowledge and belief, these are the eggs of the Yellow Rail (Coturnicops noveboracensis), the first breeding record for California, and the first set ever taken west of the Rocky Mountains."

Even Reverend Peabody, whose quests year after year are such testaments to faith and perseverance—even he was not without his share of luck. Could be, in fact, that he was blessed with it from the start, for he found his first nest at the close of his very first full day of search.

~ 9 ~

Reverend Peabody must have been a complicated man. That's your preconception, when you contemplate a minister who sought sanctuary as often in the world of birds as he did in the world of fellow men; and it's your absolute conviction, once you get to know him through his many published articles and those of his surviving letters that can be rounded up. He was a man of stark and puzzling contradictions: a humble man who could be haughty, prone to vainglory, even sanctimonious at times; a gentle, kindly man who could lacerate his fellow ornithologists stingingly for their imperfect wisdom, publicly, in print, without a second thought. He was a stern stickler for fact, who yet wrote with the ear of a musician, a painter's eye, and the soul of a romantic. He was a character, a paradox.

Reverend P.B. Peabody

Photograph courtesy of Hoslett Museum of Natural History, Decorah, Iowa.

Putnam Burton Peabody—Burton, he was called—was the son of a pioneer Episcopalian missionary. He was born in Alden, Polk County, Wisconsin, in 1856. He lived with his wife Anna, and served his father's faith, in a number of rural middle-western places: in Minnesota, during the 1890s, at Newcastle, Wyoming, until 1905; and at Kansas thereafter until he died, in 1937. About his second faith, birds (or was that his first?) he wrote constantly and copiously for all the major journals of his day, including *The Auk, The Warbler, The Osprey, The Wilson Bulletin, The Condor, Bird Lore, The Oologist,* and several others more obscure. *The Warbler* and *The Oologist,* especially, were plentifully peppered with his contributions. Usually it was the less-known and rarer birds that attracted his attentions, and his pen; and usually it was birds peculiar to the prairies. In Minnesota it was marsh hawks, and Le Conte's sparrows ("This weird, mouselike creature . . . "), and saw-whet owls and Wilson's phalaropes, among others, that caught his fancy; in Wyoming it was rock wrens, prairie falcons, and the Townsend's solitaire; in Kansas, poor-wills and Mississippi kites, and in North Dakota piping plovers, Wilson's snipe, and yellow rails. He wrote about other, more ordinary creatures, too, like horned larks and western meadowlarks, even such peculiar nonentities as the "long-tailed" chickadee and "rocky mountain" nuthatch, both now considered subspecies.

Mr. Peabody was, above all else, enthusiastic. "The genuine bird man never grows old," he wrote in 1907, in his fiftieth year. He, for one, quite surely never did. Again and again in his sketches, year after year, it is the irrepressible grown-up boy you see romping around exploring, inquiring, exclaiming.

Visualize him that way, as a "grey-haired boy"—those were his own words—and you will have him right. Imagine him, a man of thirty-eight, running downslope for a Minnesota meadow full of bobolinks, "drinking in great draughts of air," with nests in mind. . . . "The dew-gemmed grass soon drenches me, but what of that; are there not unmeasured possibilities in that same wide expanse of grass?" Or, now fifty-three, thrashing about a gooseberry patch in a "tingling fury," searching for Brewer's blackbird nests. Imagine him at seventy-one, still at it, still turning over grasses in a North Dakota coulee for that one more nest of yellow rail. Picture him that way, and you have the essential Mr. Peabody.

Sometimes in his stories he gives fond glimpses of those who were his companions in the field; like "dear, dead John C. Knox" (1909); "poor, fine John Knox" (1922), who came along to North Dakota once for yellow rails. In Wyoming there was young "Orlando, the shy, black-eyed son of a Pittsburgh millionaire" who tagged along and helped him look for prairie falcon nests, "Orlando, a quiet but most sympathetic companion." Orlando attended boarding school in Minnesota where Mr. Peabody happened to be chaplain; and he became attached to the older man, and twice invited him, two summers, to his family ranch. And there was Mr. Rolfe, in North Dakota, whom he remembers with a little eulogy, in 1930:

> *Among the many, many bird men that have wondrously befriended me in years gone by, there are few to whom I feel myself more deeply indebted than to one, Eugene Rolfe, formerly of Minnewaukan, North Dakota (but now "The Better Land," I guess).*

Usually, though, his tone is one of stubborn singularity; and he seems to savor his time alone. Certainly he had no interest in the ordinary, unaspiring spirit of ordinary human goings-on; he had only scoffs for them. Only vitriol. In Wyoming, alone one Fourth of July, he ponders the holiday festivities:

> *"It was daylight, on the Fourth of July. Family-less, for the time being, one scorned to waste the day over petty patriotic fizz and bang: he would spend the day with his Krider's Hawks.*

On the matter of nests and eggs of birds, Peabody was truly expert. Despite his self-styled amateur status, he was one of the eminent authorities of his day, and one of the more assiduous collectors, a real pioneer who often succeeded in taking rare sets of eggs that eluded others. Unlike other collectors he did not amass a large collection; rather he sold most of what he found, to enable his continued rambling and collecting. He was poor, always poor, and dependent on wealthier men, magnanimous collectors like William Leon Dawson, for the funds to continue with his work. So spare was his subsistence income that he had to ask of his friends that they send him back the cost of postage, whenever he sent along a book or other gift.

He did amass one tangible thing during all his years of studying and collecting, and that was a book manuscript, *Nesting Ways of North American Birds*. It was a monumental work, intended to fully and faithfully describe all nesting natural history for "all North American birds whose summer homes are north of the Rio Grande." For a quarter century he worked on it, ever expanding, ever revising; by 1923, nineteen years after he began, it was a tome five thousand pages long. On its behalf he was in frequent correspondence with virtually all the ornithological luminaries of the day—William Brewster, Witmer Stone, Arthur Allen, Frank Chapman, Robert Ridgway—ever seeking help with this detail or that about this species, or subspecies, or that, in whatever field of specialization the correspondent was likely to be more knowledgeable than he. He appealed to the amateur audience, with open letters in *The Oologist,* for help in filling in still other gaps.

As early as 1905, knowledge of the book was made public, by editor Lynds Jones of *The Wilson Bulletin,* who announced it to be "in preparation": "this book promises to greatly advance our knowledge of the birds along these lines, where the author is well known to be especially strong." In *The Condor,* then, in 1906, Peabody acknowledged his "forthcoming" work; and in 1911 he made a "final appeal" to *Oologist* readers, for certain specific grains of information needed before he was ready to relinquish it to "one of the two well-known eastern publishers" who had asked to read it.

But the book was never published. In 1926 he was still at it, revising it completely for the fifth time; and in 1929 he was "still reviewing, and excerpting"; but this is the last we hear of it.

In the natural sciences building at a Kansas university, third floor up, down a concrete corridor past eerie dim rooms full of white steel specimen cabinets and idle microscopes, and vapors of formaldehyde, is the drab green door of a vault. Inside are stacks of books, old books, on modular steel shelves; and on one shelf, by itself, is a small pile of effects: sundry papers, letters, three frayed notebooks, and the crumbling

pages of a photo album. They are Reverend Peabody's effects—untended, unstudied, doubtless hardly even looked at
since their donation forty years ago by a Topeka businessman.
They are a humble legacy.

Among the notebooks is one entitled *"Index," Nesting
Ways.* It is a work of some bulk itself, forty-five brittle-brown
pages long.

Among the papers is a numbered page, 5,890, typed
and signed in his own hand. *"Nesting Ways: ENDWORD"* it is
entitled; and it begins:

> *"This work is laid aside with an access of the same spir-
> it in which it was originally taken-up, namely, with an
> ever-deepening sense of the inadequacy of any one
> person for the proper completing of the tasks in-
> volved."*

And it goes on. It is his explanation. But where in the
world are the 5,889 pages that precede it? The manuscript itself is nowhere to be found.

He strove to sketch the subjects of his fancy with his
camera, too, as well as his pen. At the time, during the 1890s
and early 1900s, photography of birds was a most impractical
pursuit, a quixotic realm for dreamers, so serious were the
difficulties. Cameras were massive, clumsy contrivances made
to sit on massive wooden tripods, rock-steady, for the taking
of rock-still subjects in bright light. Films were slow, and ar-

duous to process—and, to a "plain country parson"—costly. Yet he labored at it anyway, for more than thirty years.

In 1896 there appeared a charming article by Reverend Peabody in *The Nidologist,* in three installments, entitled "The Photo Fiend." Possibly, it was the first published piece ever to grapple seriously with the problems of bird photography. Certainly, and delightfully, it sheds light on the state of photography in 1896.

In "The Photo Fiend" he draws on his own experience, which is hardly a cheery series of successes; and he coaches and cautions as well as he can any impragmatic soul who would care to follow. Beware, he says, or you too will be disappointed. Beware of the "Daylight Loading" feature of certain cameras: "Have a dark room. Load the camera there." Beware of windy days; beware of any light but the strongest sunlight. Beware of taking birds in flight:

> *I once took, in the brightest midday June sunshine, under the most favorable circumstances, with a forty-dollar camera, negative after negative of Franklin's Gulls following a prairie-breaking plow; so near me that even the most delicate shade of their colors could be distinctly seen, as they floated by, quietly and unscared, while yet in not a single negative could the uninitiated tell whether the winged things that followed the plow were bats, gnats, or cheese mites.*

It is a personable piece of writing, both jocular and erudite, entirely entertaining. And occasionally, "The Photo Fiend" bestows upon the reader some insight just as pertinent today as it was in 1896—maybe even more so: "Don't 'shoot' at everything you see; many things lose the heart of them when transferred to a negative."

It is not the entertainer, though—it is not the humorist or the wordsmith or the wit whose voice is plainest and most true in Reverend Peabody's stories about birds; it is the enthusiast, the rapt, romantic boy who scarcely can contain himself, so many and so beautiful are the wonders all around him. How beautiful, how glorious: that is all he wants to say; that is his simple, single, unapologetic lifelong theme. How beautiful, that meadowlark nest I photographed. "But oh, if only I could have photographed the song." How glorious that music of the Townsend's solitaire:

> And then, as I ardently looked and listened, as if in token that life and beauty everywhere shall ultimately triumph over death and decay, suddenly there stole forth from somewhere up the heights, mysteriously, delicately, vibrantly, a rippling song that seemed to know little of limit or of tiring. It was the song of the Solitaire.

How wondrous are even the most ordinary of Nature's things. They, too, were subjects of his caressing prose:

> What more common than the nest of the red wing? Yet I have seen one that would delight an artist's eye, the main structure of newly ripened yellow stems of early maturing grass, bent, crushed and interwoven, and lined with the delicate brown leaves of the sweet flag, fluted and ribbon-like in their withering.

But there is no question; it was for North Dakota and the "Big Coulee," and yellow rails, that Reverend Peabody saved his fondest, most poetic pen. No question, they were his dearest subjects; and to them his words returned most faithfully, again and again, especially in later years. For them, his affection was the least disguised:

> *"Here wing the Rough-legs, after meadow mice; here are wafted upon soft winds the silent and uncanny Short-eared Owls. Here in the early morning dawn of fragrant June days hoot and crow the Sharp-tailed Grouse. . . ."*

In *The Oologist,* that little magazine for fanciers of nests and eggs, he was especially revealing about how much his June trips northward meant to him. He was dependent on the funds of others for these expeditions; those of munificent Leon Dawson, in particular; and the intimate environment of this magazine was just the place to express his joy, it seems, whenever that funding was renewed. "Going again, next year? Yes, indeed!" he wrote in 1921; "Thanks to a generous bird lover of the Far West. What a fine old world this world is, anyhow." And again, in 1922: "Do any of you wonder that I long to go again, that I am boyishly flinging up my hat today at knowledge that the trip has already been financed for the June of 1922?

More than once in those *Oologist* pages, tellingly, he lapses into a possessive way of speaking about those dearest of his subjects. "My butte," "my coulee," "my beloved hilltop of boulders," "my yellow rails." He does this often and absently. He does it naturally, as one would in speaking of his family or his home. In the May, 1925 *Oologist,* at the close of a little story about his North Dakota visit of the June before, his affection rises right up and surfaces, for all to see:

*One ought not to close this brief sketch without a word
as to the little wisps of sandpipers, both large and small,
that were still to be found upon that coulee meadow,
the early days of June.*

*May I tell you of the evening when, at last, I
climbed the cow-path to the butte-crest and sat down
upon a stone for a last lingering look? And may I con-
fess it, there were tears very, very near the eye-lids, for,
had I not known and loved that very spot these twenty
years?*

That June visit to North Dakota, in 1924, was probably
his next to last.

~ 10 ~

It *bothers me, to read about* that paradisic "Big Coulee" once again, knowing it to be ploughed up and dry and gone forever. The old imagined scene returns to life with such Technicolor surety, such aura and familiarity, even though I never saw it, that I cannot accept so dismal a reality. It is more than just frustration, though to be sure there is frustration; that dismal ploughed-up reality is not only dismal, it is unconvincing. It is *too* dismal. When I think of that "most animated scene" of Mr. Peabody's telling, that valley of the past full of springs, lagoons, and disporting water birds—and then I think of the valley I found four years ago, arid and inert—I cannot reconcile the two.

Could I have missed last time? Could Mr. Peabody's paradise still be there, far from the modern road, somewhere far up the valley or down? Do I know, really *know*, that I was even close? The more I think on it, the more I wonder.

Mr. Peabody and his "Big Coulee," and the past, are not dead yet by any means. But Douglas, Manitoba, is.

Ask Del Hesse, if there's anything, or anybody, you want to know about in the region of Maddock, North Dakota. He's apt to know, and if he doesn't he's apt to help you until you do.

Maddock is the logical place to resume investigation; it is the settlement nearest that coulee of four years ago. So I roll along past town, looking for life, a place to stop and talk, and one place suggests itself, only one. Del's Store. Is anyone alive today, at Maddock? Wind whips through the empty parking lot, and down the empty street. The door is open, and I walk in. It's dim inside. Silent. In a corner, reading, deeply sunk in an old armchair is a full-grown man, and a large one, not the teenage hireling I expected. It's Del.

"I have a strange sort of question." I began reluctantly.

"And I have a strange sort of answer." Good start; he didn't miss a beat.

"Well, there was this minister from Kansas," I tell him, "and he came here ninety years ago to a place called the Big Coulee, to find a rare bird, and he came back almost every June for more than twenty years; and I want to find exactly where it was he went. I thought I found it several years ago, between here and Esmond; but now I'm not so sure. Would there be anyone alive who might remember him?"

He ponders it a minute, asks a few questions, then reaches up for the phone on the wall and dials.

"George? It's Del. Ever heard of a 'Big Coulee,' or a Reverend Peabody from Kansas?"

Nothing, obviously; he extracts himself from the conversation and dials another number.

And another, and another. He calls everyone he can think of who might be helpful, whether he knows them well or not. ("Johnny? This is Del Hesse. Your brother and I worked together on his truck, about a year ago. Ever heard of a 'Big Coulee'?")

The man is a marvel on the telephone. Smoothly, genially, swiftly, he goes from call to call with the cool of a corporate executive. At any one of a number of professions—fund-raising, selling stocks, police investigation—he would be a whiz. What an ally I have here. In a matter of minutes, he's saved me hours.

There are no immediate answers, but he has leads, ideas. Check back with me later in the day, he says. And there's a new motel in town, a half mile up the road, in case you need one.

Del's not in his chair this time; he's at the register counting change out to a man who has bought gas. With a hint of a smile he acknowledges my return, completing the transaction while I linger in the background. Two boys are next, each with a fistful of fireworks picked from a display laid out behind them on a card table.

"Got some feedback," he says, closing the cash drawer

with a bang. He walks back to his chair. There's some confu-
sion about this "Big Coulee," he tells me; there are two of
them, it seems. Two people, now, have told him that *the* "Big
Coulee," the one best known, is not the one just west of Maddock, indicated on the map, where I thought it to be; to them
the name suggests a very different place still farther west, a
deep, long valley that includes an historic site called Palmer
Springs, where encamped soldiers once were massacred by
Indians. Del knows where this is; and it's a deeper, more dramatic coulee, he says, with definite lagoons. He'll take me there
tomorrow morning.

The imperative tonight is obvious: reread those painterly paragraphs of Mr. Peabody's, in his opus of 1922. For in
them he gives landmarks:

> *In early June of a following year, 1901, I made my way*
> *across the unlinked area of rolling upland prairie, pre-*
> *cipitous ravine, and venerable butte, which lies to the*
> *west of Devil's Lake. My destination reached, I has-*
> *tened across some acres of "hog-wallow;" on over still*
> *wider area of virgin prairie, whereon disported and*
> *sang many a blithesome Longspur; and stood at last*
> *atop a great butte, looking down upon the deep-lying*
> *sea of sedges, rushes, and grasses, known locally as*
> *"The Big Coulee." In and out it wound among the hills.*

So there is a butte, and a lake to the northwest. There
are, or were, lagoons. And that stream he wrote about:

> *Far up on the top of a butte, rising out of a boggy spring*
> *pool, there flows a tiny stream of clear, sweet water.*
> *Down the slopes the streamlet flows, now losing itself*

*to view amid lush grasses, and, again, pouring itself
with noisy babbling over some buried boulder. Across
the reach of narrow, coarse-grass meadow it quietly
flows among the cowslips and sedges. Onward it meanders into the coulee; here it enlarges by intake; then
spreads wideningly and sluggishly into the broader ex-
panses. Onward, at last, the stiller waters flow.*

Rereading this old prose in my little room at Maddock,
North Dakota, so near the old place itself, yet nearly a century
away, I feel that I too have known that coulee meadow.

"How about *that*," chortles Del. The stony road before
us falls dizzyingly down a valley wall, then swoops right up the
other side. At the bottom, far down soft slopes, dark marsh
winds lazily along, bejeweled by pools—"lagoons?" The *scale*
of the place is huge—it winds away for miles. It was a "Little
Coulee" that I found four years ago. We roll down the road
slowly, bumpily; halfway down Del finds a break in a fence and
directs me through, and we drive right out on the open prairie,
following a sometime trail worn by the tires of a pickup truck.
"All virgin prairie here," says Del, who is leaning forward,
scanning, eager for what comes next. The trail meanders,
avoiding boulders, and stops at the edge of a gully. We stop,
and walk over for a look. The gully is a watercourse, of sorts,
or at least it was; between its shallow banks a fresh green
stripe of marsh steps down the slopes, expanding on the plains
below. We hear the sound of seeping water and see it, gath-
ered in little pools.

These are the "springs," Del says, of Palmer Springs, where the massacre occurred ("massacre," of course, being a word reserved for the murderous deeds of Indians only). The story is that a mail wagon under military escort was ambushed by six Sioux, who crept up and shot three soldiers dead. Two others—Palmer and his scout—escaped on their horses to Fort Totten, thirty miles away. It was only thirty-one years later, in 1899, that a young amateur oologist named Maltby wandered this North Dakota country, maybe this very slope, and discovered a nest and eggs he did not know, and sought the help of an authority in Kansas.

This could be Peabody's very stream, could it not? It runs downhill, "losing itself to view" sometimes: it babbles underground. But why would he not have cited the historic name, Palmer Springs? Who knows? The place is one a pastor would wish to write rhapsodically about, that is sure; it is a wondrous scene with its gentle light and gently sculpted hills. Below us the plain glows green, and the intermittent river glints; above us the slope climbs steeply upward to a windy sky.

Right overhead, ten yards above us, hanging in the wind with trembling wings, is an upland sandpiper, a beautiful thing to see. He tips his head back to the sky and with all his might, all his body's breath, he pours out all his melancholy song, which drifts out across and down the valley, fades, then hauntingly returns in echo. Not so long ago the mournful magic of this prairie song had all but vanished from the plains of North Dakota, and elsewhere; like all the other shorebirds, all the other birds and animals of North America that were both plentiful and obvious enough to shoot, they were shot, and they were decimated. By 1920 the upland "plover," as it then was called (with happy euphony, the smooth, round sound of "plover" befitting beautifully a bird of "dove"-like sculpture)— the upland plover had become a rarity in North Dakota. "Sad to relate, not an upland plover did I find, in all that early June sojourn," wrote Reverend Peabody of his visit that year. "This is the first experience of that sort in fifteen years." Just two years later, in 1922, he wrote that it was "heard no more." But three-quarters of a century later it is back and common once again, one of the luckier of birds.

Not two hours have passed and I'm right back here at Palmer Springs, alone this time, to explore that springy marsh that flows down the slopes. It's a quaking, boggy sort of marsh; it shudders like pudding when you walk on it. And the grass, the *green* of it: it is unlike that of any other I ever saw, so clean and bright as to seem unnatural. Tangibly it is different too, weighty yet fine, like long, heavy hair, a sensuous pleasure to sift through with your hands. But I don't think this down-flowing little meadow is big enough, *wide* enough that is, for rails. Downslope it does broaden, though; maybe there is room down there. I'll work my way down.

This is, surely, "a most animated scene," no doubt of that. Below, in the lagoons and in the reeds, it is boiling with birds. Ducks come and go—teals of both kinds, and larger ones; coots bleat and grebes make gulping calls, and marsh wrens sing ebulliently, ever-optimistically, undiscouraged by the squealing clamor of the blackbirds, yellow-heads, and red-wings, many hundreds of them in the reeds. Black terns course about and stop, hawk-like, to hover, and snipes overhead are continuously streaking by like missiles, making windy music. When after many minutes of this showmanship they tire, they hold back their wings and fall to the earth bill-first, like darts.

Up on the slopes all kinds of birds are singing: western meadowlarks, ventriloquial and difficult to see, though they are usually plainly perched; and unseen buzzing sparrows, clay-colored, grasshopper, and savannah, and very likely Bairds, though I am not so sure. Best of all are those brave birds that proclaim their songs aflight, openly, with ardor un-concealed, like the chestnut-colored longspurs, which sing meadowlark-like songs, and boisterous lark buntings, ever upward-swooping and then coasting, parachuting down with wings held high, and piping loudly; and upland sandpipers, aeolian, sad, and somewhere far away. Melancholy, gay, whis-per-thin: how varied are these songs of prairie birds. Yet equally they all belong here in the open, in the wind, upon these wispy slopes; all are inextricable from their prairie home as the fluting songs of thrushes are from forest dark.

What havens these coulees are. Where else can you find this intimate adjacency of marsh and prairie birds? At the one hand are the riotous water birds; at the other, the solitary songs of open spaces: in one ear you have the tomfoolery of squawking, splashing ducks and coots, and in the other the windy songs of sparrows and meadowlarks and longspurs. Where else would it be so, with such ensured proximity? There is one other beautiful thing about these North Dakota coulees, and that is the unbroken native prairie that lies intact upon their flanks. Seldom anymore do prairie birds still sing in pris-tine prairie homes, but here they do, on these lonesome coulee slopes; here they sing in a setting materially unchanged since meltwaters of receding glaciers ceased their cutting of the valleys and subsided, ten or twenty thousand years ago. Random boulders lie unaltered, in their original Pleistocene arrangements. It's nice to know, and nice to think about.

And there is yet another beautiful thing about these coulees: there are no boundaries, or rules. Where else would you be at such liberty to enjoy these birds, in such a pristine setting? They are refuges, to be sure—not Refuges, however. Too small and fragmentary for federal recognition, they are left in the hands of private owners, farmers who make light use of them as grazing land for cattle. So, you are denied, or rather spared, the amenities of the National Wildlife Refuges— the visitor centers with flush toilets and interpretive brochures and maps, and staff to answer questions; the observation towers, boardwalks, nature trails, and periodic guided tours, and auto routes along dikes with signs posted along the way to tell you where to stop, and what to see, and what the annual duck production is in thousands; signs to label the exhibits, in other words. They are really just museums, these Refuges; just open-air museums. Or cageless zoos, if you prefer, for the exhibits *are* alive.

In a Wildlife Refuge the feeling that pervades is one of management. It is all planned, you sense, not wild; it is merely delegated space where plants and birds are permitted and provided for, like Indians on a reservation. One more precinct of man, that's all.

Of course, the feeling that pervades is one of regulation. Heaven forfend that you should wish to wander away from the car, or trail, and out into a marsh and discover things, take

photographs; there are frowns for that, and permits necessary. Of course it has to be so, or little boys would harass the
birds, and bigger boys would shoot them.

So you go elsewhere, if you don't like it. You go to
places like this North Dakota coulee, where you can wander
your own solipsistic way as long and as far and as inquisitive-
ly as you please, carefree as a child. You find your own refuge,
your own wilderness uncharted and uncensused by any scientist, unstripped of its surprises. *Nobody knows* which sparrows nest upon these grassy hills, which rails or bitterns in
this marsh; and so it is worth searching, worth finding out.

Intrusion. Up the hill a pickup truck pulls up beside my
car. So much for solipsism. Two men get out. And they stand,
watch, and no doubt wonder what in the world I'm doing
down here in this marsh, turning the grasses over with a stick.
They start ambling down the slope. I know what will happen
now; they'll tell me that I'm trespassing.

But no, they're only curious. They graze some cattle up
this valley, and were driving by and saw the car and its foreign
license plate. Thought I might be here for artifacts. Leon
Arnold is the name; and with him is Len, his son.

Well no, I'm here for birds, not artifacts, I tell them.
They are so open and friendly that my usual reticence is un-
necessary, even undesirable, I sense. I tell them about the Reverend and the "Big Coulee," and the bird that hides in marshes
and sounds like a typewriter when it calls.

"Like a *typewriter?*" Leon's eyes open wide, then narrow a little with incredulity.

"That grass you're standing in," he says, after a moment
of reflection, "I know where there's lots of it. Twenty acres of

it. Grows where it's all wet and spongy and shaky when you walk on it."

How true. "And where is that?" I ask.

"That's up on Trapper's Coulee. We have a farm up there. Why there's more birds out in that place, when you go out there in the evening . . . it's kind of nice, you know?"

His voice is that of a man who really likes it out there in the evening, with all the birds. You can tell.

"You ought to talk with Clarence Jensen," he adds, after another moment of reflection. "Lives in Esmond. He's ninety-one years old and sharp as a tack, remembers everything. He'd know about your Reverend Peabody, if anybody would."

We chat by a barbed wire fence, me on one side and the Arnolds on the other. This whole Cheyenne valley, for nearly twenty miles, is known as the "Big Coulee," Leon says. He'll take me out to see that spongy, grassy place sometime, he says, if I want to go. Just let him know. And I *should* see Clarence Jensen.

What commands your attention when you drive in to Esmond is not the Trinity Lutheran Church spire, though it certainly strives for it; it is a huge steel water tank held high above the town by a framework of pipes and braces: a crude, utilitarian affair compared to those bulbous designer jobs with wineglass stems you see in lands of prospering technology, like Delaware and New Jersey. ESMOND, it says, in plain no-nonsense lettering. No nonsense: that is the Esmond theme; it is conveyed all around you, by the plain brick school,

Esmond, North Dakota

the small sufficient houses, the plain brick post office distin-
guished only by its waving flag. No excess, no decoration, no
nonsense; just pure utility. Esmond does provide a public pay
phone, though, and a modern one at that, of the talk-right-
from-your-car variety. I spot it right away, in the lot of an abandoned service station. Across the lot, by the gas pumps, a light
fixture is broken off and dangling and banging in the wind.

The phone rings twice, and Mr. Jensen answers. Well,
here we go again: I'm interested in a minister from Kansas, I
tell him, who came here years ago . . .

"Peabody," he says.

Could I come over for a talk?

Mr. Jensen's is not a fancy neighborhood; the drive-
ways and the road that serves it are only dirt, and the yards
and houses are very small. But it is snug and friendly, homey;
lawns are neat and green, and gardens full of flowers. I find
him waiting on the lawn, by his bright red house. He is skinny,
and stands a little crooked, and wears a baseball cap.

Did he know Rev. P.B. Peabody? Ever meet him in the
flesh? No, he never did, but there was ample talk about the
man, he remembers, when he was a little boy. He remembers
something Peabody was alleged to say: "And there was the
nest of a yellow rail." He reenacts it slowly, with drama, ges-
ticulating as he does.

Where did Mr. Peabody stay? Right over there, with
the Dickeys—he points diagonally across the street. Mr. and
Mrs. G.H. Dickey. She was something of a naturalist, he says;
she especially liked to garden. Now all the Dickeys are dead
and gone.

Mr. Jensen is a lucid man at ninety-one.

Clarence Jensen

He thinks that Peabody found his rails not in the "Big Coulee" but in Trapper's Coulee, a lesser tributary coulee, or in one of *its* tributary coulees close to Esmond. He suggests we go for a drive, so he can show me where he means.

Life in Esmond has its compensations, apparently, for Clarence has lived here all his life, except for a stint of several years he spent traveling as a baseball player in the professional minor leagues. He pitched. Had a curve ball and a knuckle ball but no slider: nobody had one in those days. Knew Yogi Berra for a while. Then he came back to Esmond and married, and settled, and taught school. He is alone, now that his wife has died. Under a black, apocalyptic sky, just south of what must be an awful storm, my friend points out these tributary coulees. They're pretty places, all of them, smooth little valleys, but they are all too dry. No sponginess, no standing water. Trapper's Coulee itself is inaccessible by road, he says. "Your best bet there is Leon Arnold. Ask him to take you in his truck."

It's nothing new to Leon; he does it every day. But to me it's exhilarating, bounding over the prairie high in the cab of a pickup truck; up over humps we go, and down through hollows and through tall grass and up again, then smoothly we cruise the short-grass plain. Leon, too, has lived here all his life; his father too before him. He knows intimately every single acre of his land, and there are thousands of them. "It's country you kind of get attached to," he says, in his usual understated way. Dusk is closing in; we'll not have too much time.

There are certain clues, certain features of the land, I tell

Leon, that might help solve this coulee mystery: a lake to the northwest, an overlooking butte and lagoons, and a spring that runs downhill—do any of these jibe with your boggy, spongy place? Any of these familiar? The word "butte" confounds him. "Can't think of one," he says. "They have those farther west, not here." "Lagoons," too, sound foreign. But there is a spring that runs down a hill, he says. He'll show me. We drive on through the grass, and through the dusk.

"OK, let's walk." Leon brakes to a stop and we jump out. It is a place of perfect and unearthly stillness: fog hangs motionless above a meadow, far out into the distance. But there is much to hear out there, in all that stillness: sedge wrens. The meadow must be full of them. This is good, Leon, I say; where you have these wrens you might have yellow rails. The stream? He shows me. It has been dammed, and there is a little pond, and under ground then, he says, it seeps out into the meadow.

Out we go, right into that spongy meadow. Leon leads the way. Spongy, yes, and gurgling, and the water is *cold*— Leon has heavy leather boots, but I have only sneakers. It shudders, too. It is indeed a bog—or to be precise a "fen," because it is in a region of limy soils—just as he had said; and it is full of that very same fleshy grass he found me in this morning at Palmer Springs. "Listen!" I stop Leon in his tracks. A yellow rail is snapping fifty feet away.

"Like a *typewriter*," he says, after a moment of gradual cognition. "It does sound like a typewriter!" He looks at me with big round eyes.

"Like a *typewriter*." He repeats it, as we drive back over the prairie through the dusk. He really can't get over that. And

Leon Arnold

the fact that we really heard it equally astounds him; and it does me too, but I'm still perplexed. Where is the overlooking butte? To be sure it is a "sea of grass," but a *"deep-lying"* sea of grass? And what of the lagoons, and the glistening lake? Leon has no answers.

That spongy bog of Leon's, if I have it right, is at the very confluence of two coulees, "Big Coulee" and Trapper's Coulee. This morning my idea is to get a look at the scene from far away, to the south, from the far side of the "Big Coulee," a mile or more away. I find just the access that I'm looking for, too, four miles south of Esmond, a grid road that slashes right across the major coulee well to the south of Trapper's. Right here, where it crosses, the coulee is narrow, and for the most part dry, a grassy trough. Often in these Benson County coulees the water disappears underground and does not reappear for miles; Clarence Jensen told me so.

I drive across and park the car and scramble up a sandy hill, then down and up another. And there it all is: below, and stretching northward far away, is the "Big Coulee," a waterless river full of swaying grass. Along the near side, the western side, not far away, is a string of bright blue ponds, dark ducks afloat upon them. Way up there to the north is what must be Trapper's Coulee, a great gouge in the horizon. Here the "Big Coulee" turns to the northwest, toward what the map calls Buffalo Lake, which is visible and shining. It's such a beautiful day. The sun is hot, the breeze alive, and cool; titanic clouds like great white arctic masses tower above the summer plain.

Their undersides parallel perfectly the prairie they ride across, as if worn flat by their glacial journey. It is a breathless scene. I run back over the hillocks to the car, for my big camera, the four-by-five, and tripod and film holders and focusing cloth; and thus burdened I hobble back and set up hurriedly, before it all drifts away. It all depends on these clouds. Here on these northern plains the clouds alone can decide a photograph.

It is the northward view that captures me, with its particular drama. On the ground glass I fill my scene entirely with sky, except for a sliver of horizon at the bottom that includes that region of Trapper's Coulee, and I assemble it just so, and level it . . . and I notice something. That high plain between the two coulees, where they diverge: it is a "butte," you might say, if you came from Kansas. Well, there is a lake "to the northwest" all right—Buffalo Lake—and the lagoons, of course, those strung-together ponds below! It dawns on me. That "butte" is just exactly where Mr. Peabody stood and first beheld the scene, one June day long ago. Below it, in Leon's springy, spongy meadow, is where he spent his days with yellow rails.

I've found it.

Speedily I snap two pictures of my waiting clouds, then pack up and scramble back down and up and down the hillocks. I drive back down that grid road in the direction of Leon's farm, with a tail of dust behind the car. But, in my haste I make a wrong turn, or two wrong turns, I don't know; these grid roads all look the same. The landscape, too, all looks the same. Far up ahead a pickup truck is fast approaching. Maybe he'll stop, if I pull over and roll my window down and look confused. I do, and he does. He rolls his window down and leans out: "I've been *looking* for you," he says. It's Leon.

He was looking for *me*.

"I've been thinking, and I've got it figured out . . . "

"The butte." I interrupt him. "I know where it is."

"So do I. Hop in, and I'll take you there right now."

Off we go in his truck again, for another of those jouncy rides. He cuts back across the countryside on grid roads, toward town; on one rutty downhill stretch he stops—inexplicably, for there is no other road to take—then he pulls off and drives right over the prairie on a faded road, which fades away altogether soon, but that does not slow us down; at speed we continue through waist-high grass that abrades the undercarriage audibly, shrilly, no doubt brushing it very, very clean, if not burnishing bare metal to a shine. Before us, a rain of crickets is raised by our violent passage. They pour over us in all kinds, all sizes, all possible permutations of yellow and brown and green. Some ride the hood in front of us, displayed in assortments ever-changing; continuously they snap away, and just as continuously they are replaced by other startled passengers. This close, the ceramic chitin of their armor gleams.

I ask Leon if it hurts his truck, tearing through the grass like this. No, he says; but you have to back-flush the radiator often, with a high-pressure water hose, to blow the grass seed out, or the engine will overheat. Otherwise it does no harm.

A change lies just ahead, just over the grass. I feel it. We've come to the end of the earth, it seems. Beyond, the scene is painterly and faint. And below—we stop, jump out, and walk over for a look—below us, far down windy slopes, deep-lying, is a churning sea of grass. Due south, dotted by shrubs, is Leon's bog. He points it out.

How fine a stroke of luck it was, meeting Leon down

there at Palmer Springs, just yesterday morning was it? I might be down there still, benighted and still searching, had he not just happened by, and been curious. The *coincidence*. I thank him for his help, but he shrugs it off.

"It's been fun," he says, abashedly. "But it happened so *fast*." I think he'd like our mystery to have lasted a little longer. His attention fades away, is lost.

I think of all that has happened to North Dakota, and the world, since the minister from Kansas stood here ninety years ago. All the roads were made of dirt and all the carriages had horses, when he first looked out upon this sea of grass. In an age of agribusiness and superhighways and gleaming office parks it ought to seem a miracle, that this coulee and these rails survive. But somehow it does not.

As we talk the wind keens and curses, and catches swallows, and sends them speeding past; and the meadow roils below; and through the wind distinctly, insistently, there comes the pattering of yellow rails. They are still down there, still beckoning after all those years. Of course they are.

BIBLIOGRAPHY

Allen, J.A. 1900. The Little Black Rail. *Auk.* 17: 1–8.

Audubon, John James. 1840. *The Birds of America.*

Barrett, Bruce. 1977. Yellow Rail, Bohemian Waxwing / Ottawa, Canada. *Birding.* 9: 112.

Bent, Arthur Cleveland. 1926. *Life Histories of North American Marsh Birds.* Washington: National Museum Bulletin. 135.

Brownstein, Richard. 1972. Yellow Rail / Douglas, Manitoba. *Birding* 4:21.

Clark, John N. 1884. Nesting of the Little Black Rail in Connecticut. *Auk.* 1: 393–4.

—— 1897. The Little Black Rail. *The Nidologist.* 4: 86–9.

Cobb, Stanley. 1906. A Little Black Rail in Massachusetts. *Bird Lore.* 8: 136–7.

Dear, L.S. 1938. Yellow Rail at Churchill, Manitoba. *Auk.* 55: 670–1.

Devitt, Otto E. 1939. The Yellow Rail Breeding in Ontario. *Auk.* 56: 238–243.

Elliott, R.D. and Morrison, R.I.S. 1979. The Incubation Period of the Yellow Rail. *Auk.* 96: 422–3.

Faanes, Craig A. 1981. Northern Great Plains Region. *American Birds* 35:953.

———— 1984. Yellow Rail / Benson County, North Dakota. *Birding* 16: 118.

———— 1985. Northern Great Plains Region. *American Birds.* 39: 929.

Forbush, Edward Howe. 1912. *A History of the Game Birds, Wild Fowl and Shorebirds of Massachusetts and Adjacent States.* Boston: Massachusetts State Board of Agriculture.

Gosse, Philip Henry. 1847. *Birds of Jamaica.* London: John Van Voorst.

Harlow, Richard C. 1913. Nesting of the Black Rail (*Cresciscus jamaicensis)* in New Jersey. *Auk.* 30: 269.

Hickey, Joseph L. 1965. On Finding Black Rail Nests. *Linnaean News Letter.* May.

Huber, Ronald. 1959. Yellow Rails in Becker and Mahnomen Counties, Minnesota. *The Flicker.* September: 82–3.

Janssen, Robert B. 1971. Yellow Rail / Mahnomen, Minnesota. *Birding.* 3x.

———— 1973. Western Great Lakes Region. *American Birds.* 27: 872.

Jones, Ian. 1982. Nesting of the Yellow Rail at Richmond Fen. *The Shrike.* Nov-Dec.: 3.

Lane, John, 1962. Nesting of the Yellow Rail in Southwestern Manitoba. *The Canadian Field Naturalist.* 76: 189–191.

Maltby, Fred. 1915. Nesting of the Yellow Rail in North Dakota. *The Oologist.* 32: 122–4.

Meanley, Brooke. 1975. *Birds and Marshes of the Chesapeake Bay Country.* Centreville, Md.: Tidewater.

Nauman, E.D. 1927. Notes on the Rails. *The Wilson Bulletin.* 39: 217–218.

*Peabody, Reverend P.B. 1895. Dragging for Bobolinks. *The Oologist.* 12: 123–126.

———— 1896. The Photo Fiend. *The Nidologist.* 3: 85–86, 97–98, 126–129.

———— 1897. Song Notes and Nesting Notes of the Western Meadowlark. *The Osprey.* 1: 139–141.

———— 1901. Nesting Habits of Le Conte's Sparrow. *The Auk.* 18: 129–134.

———— 1905. The Nesting of the Yellow Rail. *The Warbler.* 1: 49–51.

———— 1907. The Prairie Falcons of Saddleback Butte. *The Condor.* 9: 180–184.

———— 1908. Krideri the Fearless. *The Warbler.* 4: 1–8.

———— 1909. The Bleating and Breeding of the Snipe. *The Warbler.* 5: 2–7.

———— 1909. Cyanocephalus the Obscure. *The Warbler.* 5: 15–20.

———— 1910. Nesting of the King Rail. *The Oologist.* 27: 90–91.

———— 1911. Wanted: Reliable Information. *The Oologist.* 28: 59.

———— 1920. North Dakota Birds of Coulee and Moraine. *The Oologist.* 37: 93–95.

*A *selected* bibliography: of the scores of Reverend Peabody's articles consulted, only those most pertinent to the text of *Shadowbirds* are listed here.

——— 1922. Haunts and Breeding Habits of the Yellow Rail. *Journal of the Museum of Comparative Oology*. 2: 33–44.

——— 1922. Birds Among the Buttes. *The Oologist*. 39: 170–173.

——— 1925. Belated. *The Oologist*. 42: 74–76.

——— 1933. The Piping Plover. *The Oologist*. 50: 160–161.

——— 1935. Rimrock and Solitaire. *The Wilson Bulletin*. 47: 257–265.

Post, William and Enders, Frank. 1969. Reappearance of the Black Rail on Long Island. *Kingbird*. 19: 189–191.

Reynard, George B. 1974. Some Vocalizations of the Black, Yellow, and Virginia Rails. *Auk*. 91: 747–756.

Ripley, S. Dillon. 1977. *Rails of the World*. Boston: David R. Godine.

Savaloja, Terry. 1975. Yellow Rail / Hassman, Minnesota. *Birding*. March: 97.

Sprunt, Alexander, Jr. 1954. *Florida Bird Life*. New York: Coward-Mc Cann.

Stalheim, Philip Scott. 1974. *Behavior and Ecology of the Yellow Rail (Coturnicops noveboracensis)*. Unpublished: Master's Thesis, University of Minnesota.

——— 1975. Breeding and Behavior of Captive Yellow Rails. *Aviculture Magazine*. 81: 133–141.

Stenzel, Jeffrey R. 1982. *Ecology of Breeding Yellow Rails at Seney National Wildlife Refuge*. Unpublished: Master's Thesis, Ohio State University.

Stewart, Robert E. and Robbins, Chandler S. 1958. *Birds of Maryland and the District of Columbia*. Washington: U.S. Dept. of the Interior, Fish and Wildlife Service.

Terril, L.M.C.I. 1943. Nesting Habits of the Yellow Rail in Gaspé County, Québec. *Auk*. 60: 171–180.

Thoreau, Henry David. *Journal:* May 10, 1853.

Walkinshaw, Lawrence. 1939. The Yellow Rail in Michigan. *Auk.* 56: 227–237.

Wayne, Arthur T. 1905. Breeding of the Little Black Rail, *Porzana jamaicensis* in South Carolina. *The Warbler.* 1: 33–35.

Weske, John S. 1979. *An Ecological Study of the Black Rail in Dorchester County, Maryland.* Unpublished: Master's Thesis, Cornell University.

INDEX